PERL

Quick Reference

PERL

Quick Reference

Mícheál Ó Foghlú

QUE®

Perl Quick Reference
 For information, address Que Corporation, 201 W. 103rd Street, Indianapolis, IN, 46290. You may reach Que's direct sales line by calling 1-800-428-5331.

Library of Congress Catalog No.: 96-69949

ISBN: 0-7897-0888-4

98 97 96 6 5 4 3 2

Interpretation of the printing code: the rightmost double-digit number is the year of the book's printing; the rightmost single-digit number, the number of the book's printing. For example, a printing code of 96-1 shows that the first printing of the book occurred in 1996.

Credits

President
Roland Elgey

Publisher
Joseph B. Wikert

Publishing Manager
Fred Slone

Senior Title Manager
Bryan Gambrel

Editorial Services Director
Elizabeth Keaffaber

Managing Editor
Sandy Doell

Director of Marketing
Lynn E. Zingraf

Acquisitions Editor
Al Valvano

Production Editor
Patrick Kanouse

Editors
Elizabeth Barrett
Jeff Riley

Product Marketing Manager
Kim Margolius

Assistant Product Marketing Manager
Christy M. Miller

Strategic Marketing Manager
Barry Pruett

Technical Editor
Joe Milton

Technical Support Specialist
Nadeem Muhammed

Acquisitions Coordinator
Carmen Krikorian

Software Relations Coordinator
Patty Brooks

Editorial Assistant
Andrea Duvall

Book Designer
Ruth Harvey

Cover Designer
Nathan Clement

Production Team
Marcia Brizendine
Jenny Earhart
Joan Evan
DiMonique Ford
Amy Gornik
Staci Somers

Indexer
Becky Hornyak

Composed in Frutiger and ITC Kabel by Que Corporation.

This book is dedicated to my mother, Máire Foley, who bought me my first computer (and didn't laugh too hard when the library system I developed could only hold details on three books); and also to my father, Michael John Pats Phaddy Amhlaoibh Ó Foghlú, who taught me the value of books and the importance of names.

About the Author

Mícheál Ó Foghlú is now a lecturer in Applied Computing and Information Systems in Waterford Regional Technical College, Ireland (**http://www.rtc-waterford.ie**). Until September 1996, he was working in the Computer Services department in University College Galway, Ireland (**http://www.ucg.ie**). His interests include Natural Language Processing, WWW programming and development, Linux, computing using the Irish language, and Z39.50. When not slaving over a hot computer, he is sometimes seen nursing a quiet pint while listening to loud Irish music, or meandering through the hills in no particular direction.

He can be contacted **ofoghlu@indigo.ie**.

Acknowledgments

I would like to thank all my colleagues in the Computer Services department in UCG, especially Paul Doyle and Sinéad N' Fhaoláin, for bearing with me. Thanks are also due to all the Que team for their cooperation and help in the production of this book. Though I do not know him personally, I would like to thank Larry Wall for contributing Perl to the rest of us!

We'd Like to Hear from You!

As part of our continuing effort to produce books of the highest possible quality, Que would like to hear your comments. To stay competitive, we *really* want you, as a computer book reader and user, to let us know what you like or dislike most about this book or other Que products.

You can mail comments, ideas, or suggestions for improving future editions to the address below, or send us a fax at (317) 581-4663. For the online inclined, Macmillan Computer Publishing has a forum on CompuServe (type **GO QUEBOOKS** at any prompt) through which our staff and authors are available for questions and comments. The address of our Internet site is **http://www.mcp.com** (World Wide Web).

In addition to exploring our forum, please feel free to contact me personally to discuss your opinions of this book: I'm **74670,3710** on CompuServe, and I'm **avalvano@que.mcp.com** on the Internet.

Thanks in advance—your comments will help us to continue publishing the best books available on computer topics in today's market.

Al Valvano
Product Development Specialist
Que Corporation
201 W. 103rd. Street
Indianapolis, Indiana 46290
USA

Contents at a Glance

Table of Contents

Contents

INTRODUCTION

This book is a reference guide for the programming language called Perl. This book does not describe how to install Perl on your computer; if you do not already have Perl installed, this book will not be very useful!

Note If you want to install Perl and have access to the Internet visit the Central Perl Archive Network (CPAN). The master site is at **ftp://ftp.funet.fi/pub/languages/perl/CPAN/**, and there are many mirror sites around the world. This is as much as can be found on Perl installation in this guide!

Perl has many uses, especially in UNIX system administrative tasks, which is where Perl was born and grew up. The name stands for "Practical Extraction and Report Language." Nowadays, Perl is seen by many as the ideal development language for Web server scripts.

This chapter describes the advantages of using Perl and outlines the structure of *Perl Quick Reference*.

Why Use Perl?

People use Perl because it is quick, efficient, and easy to maintain when programming a wide range of tasks, in particular those involving the manipulation of text files. Also, there are many others also using Perl who are prepared to share their code.

Rapid Development

Many programming projects are high level rather than low level. That means that they tend not to involve bit-level manipulations, direct operating system calls. Instead, they focus on reading from files, reformatting the output, and writing it to standard output—for example, a Web browser. With Perl, the programmer does not need to get involved in the details of how file handles and buffers are manipulated, how memory is allocated, and so on. You can tell it to slurp in the contents of a file and display it on the standard output device but with all newlines replaced by tabs:

```
while ( <INFILE> )  {  s/\n/\t/;  print;  }
```

Let's not worry about the details of what's happening in that code example until the "Perl Overview" chapter. Just notice two things:

- It's very short.
- It's almost legible even without knowing any Perl, especially if you are familiar with C.

In a nutshell, that's the secret to rapid development: Write small amounts of powerful code without having to pause to consider awkward issues of syntax at every step.

Perl is pithy; a little Perl code goes a long way. In terms of programming languages, that usually means that the code will be difficult to read and painful to write. But although Larry Wall, the author of Perl, says that Perl is functional rather than elegant, most programmers quickly find that Perl code is very readable and that it is not difficult to become fluent at writing it. This is especially true of the high-level, macro operations typically required in Web development.

As it happens, Perl is quite capable of handling some pretty low-level operations, too. It can handle operating system signals and talk to network sockets, for example.

Compiler and Interpreter

A program by itself can't achieve anything. To carry out its work, it needs to be fed to either a compiler or an interpreter. Both have their advantages:

- A compiler takes a program listing and generates an executable file. This executable file can then be executed as many times as necessary, copied to other computers, and so on without the need for the program source code. This helps to keep program details confidential.

  Because the compiler only runs once, it can afford to take its time about generating the executable code. As a result, compilers tend to perform elaborate optimization on the program code with the result that the executable code runs very efficiently.
- An interpreter examines a program listing line by line and carries out the tasks required by the code there and then. There is no need for a separate compilation stage; once the program has

been written, it can be executed without delay. This makes for a rapid development cycle.

There are advantages and disadvantages to both approaches. Compiled code takes longer to prepare, but then it runs fast and your source stays secret. Interpreted code gets up and running quickly but isn't as fast as interpreted code. You also need to distribute the program source code if you want to allow others to run your programs.

So which of these categories describes Perl?

Well, Perl is a little special in this regard; it is a compiler that thinks it's an interpreter. Perl compiles program code into executable code before running it, so there is an optimization stage and the executable code runs quickly. However, it doesn't write this code to a separate executable file. Instead, it stores it in memory and then executes it.

This means that Perl combines the rapid development cycle of an interpreted language with the efficient execution of compiled code. The corresponding disadvantages are also there, though: The need to compile the program each time it runs means a slower startup than a purely compiled language and requires developers to distribute source code to users.

In practice, these disadvantages are not too limiting. The compilation phase is extremely fast, so you're unlikely to notice much of a lag between invoking a Perl script and the start of execution.

In summary, Perl is compiled "behind the scenes" for rapid execution, but you can treat it as if it is interpreted. This makes it easy for you to tweak your HTML; just edit the code and let the users run it. But is that good programming practice? Hey, that's one for the philosophers.

Flexibility

Perl was not designed in the abstract. It was written to solve a particular problem and it evolved to serve an ever widening set of real-world problems.

It could have been expanded to handle these tasks by adding more and more keywords and operators, hence making the language bigger. Instead, the core of the Perl language started out small and became more refined as time went on. In some ways, it actually contracted; the number of reserved words in Perl 5 is actually less than half the number in Perl 4, not more.

This reflects an awareness that Perl's power lies in it's unique combination of efficiency and flexibility. Perl itself has grown slowly and thoughtfully, usually in ways that allow for enhancements and extensions to be added on rather than being hard-wired in. This approach has been critical in the development of Perl's extensibility over time, as the next section explains.

Extensibility

Much of the growth in Perl as a platform has come by way of the increasing use of libraries (Perl 4) and modules (Perl 5). These are mechanisms that allow developers to write self-contained portions of Perl code that can be slotted in to a Perl application.

These add-ons range from fairly high-level utilities, such as a module that adds HTML tags to text, to low-level, down-and-dirty development tools such as code profilers and debuggers.

The ability to use extensions like these is a remarkable advance in the development of a fairly slick language, and it has helped to fuel the growth in Perl use. It makes it easy for Perl developers to share their work with others; the arrival of objects in Perl 5 makes structured design methodologies possible for Perl applications. The language has come of age without loosing any of its flexibility or raw power.

Web Server Scripts

Web servers generate huge amounts of HTML. The "M" stands for "Markup," and you need lots of it to make your Web pages look more exciting than the average insurance contract. It's an awkward business though, with problems arising easily if tags are misplaced or misspelled. Perl is a good choice of language to look after the details for you while you get on with the big picture. This is especially true if you call on Perl 5's object-oriented capabilities.

Another facet of Perl that is of particular interest to many Web server managers is that Perl works very well with standard UNIX DBM files and support for proprietary databases is growing. This is a significant consideration if you plan to allow users to query database material over the Web.

Security

Security is a major issue when writing system administrative programs and on the Internet in general. Using Perl for scripting on your Web server, you can easily guard against users trying to sneak commands through for the server to execute on their behalf. There is also an excellent Perl 5 module called `pgpperl`, also known as Penguin, that allows your server to use public-key cryptography techniques to guard sensitive data from eavesdroppers.

Ubiquity

Lots of people on the Web already use Perl! Going with the flow isn't always the best approach, but Perl has grown with the Web. There is a lot of experience out there if you need advice. The Perl developers are keenly aware of Web issues as they add to Perl. And many Perl modules have been built with the Web specially in mind.

Why You Want to Use Perl

There are many reasons why you want to use Perl. It is small, efficient, flexible, and robust. Perl is particularly well suited for Web development work where text output is a major preoccupation. If the reasons previously outlined aren't quite enough, consider this: Perl is completely free.

The Structure of This Book

This book falls clearly into two parts. Part 1 is a discursive overview of the Perl language, describing some things that are not easily summarized in tables. Part 2 is a set of reference chapters that describes the various aspects of Perl in detail.

- "Perl Overview," describes all the features of Perl in a discursive manner. This chapter introduces the basic concepts of programming in Perl. Some things are not easily summarized in tabular form, even in a quick reference guide, which is why this chapter is included.
- "Perl Reference," covers all Perl variables, operators, and functions in detail. Each of these subsections are arranged in a format that makes it easy to locate an item for reference. Icons mark each variable, operator, and function as being available in Perl 4, Perl 5, and NT Perl (the hip communications Win32 port).
- "Reference Tables" summarizes regular expressions and lists the standard Perl 5 modules.

- A glossary of terms used in this book that may be unfamiliar.
- A detailed index.

PERL OVERVIEW

Perl Quick Reference is designed as a reference guide for the Perl language, rather than an introductory text. However, there are some aspects of the language that are better summarized in a short paragraph as opposed to a table in a reference section. Therefore, this part of the book puts the reference material in context giving an overview of the Perl language, in general.

Running Perl

The simplest way to run a Perl program is to invoke the Perl interpreter with the name of the Perl program as an argument:

```
perl sample.pl
```

The name of the Perl file is `sample.pl`, and `perl` is the name of the Perl interpreter. This example assumes that Perl is in the execution path; if not, you will need to supply the full path to Perl, too:

```
/usr/local/hin/perl sample.pl
```

This is the preferred way of invoking Perl because it eliminates the possibility that you might accidentally invoke a copy of Perl other than the one you intended. We will use the full path from now on to avoid any confusion.

This type of invocation is the same on all systems with a command-line interface. The following line will do the trick on Windows NT, for example:

```
c:\NTperl\perl sample.pl
```

Invoking Perl on UNIX

UNIX systems have another way to invoke an interpreter on a script file. Place a line like

```
#!/usr/local/bin/perl
```

at the start of the Perl file. This tells UNIX that the rest of this script file is to be interpreted by `/usr/local/bin/perl`. Then make the script itself executable:

```
chmod +x sample.pl
```

You can then "execute" the script file directly and let the script file tell the operating system what interpreter to use while running it.

Invoking Perl on Windows NT

Windows NT, on the other hand, is quite different. You can use File Manager (Explorer under Windows NT 4 or Windows 95) to create an association between the file extension .PL and the Perl executable. Whenever a file ending in .PL is invoked, Windows will know that Perl should be used to interpret it.

Command-Line Arguments

Perl takes a number of optional command-line arguments for various purposes. These are listed in table 1. Most are rarely used but are given here for reference purposes.

Table 1 Perl 5 Command-Line Switches

Option	Arguments	Purpose	Notes
`-0`	octal character code	Specify record separator	Default is newline (`\n`)
`-a`	none	Automatically split records	Used with `-n` or or `-p`
`-c`	none	Check syntax only	Do not execute

Option	Arguments	Purpose	Notes
`-d`	none	Run script using Perl debugger	If Perl debugging option was included when Perl was installed
`-D`	flags	Specify debugging behavior	See table 2
`-e`	command	Pass a command to Perl from the command line	Useful for quick operations
`-F`	regular expression	If `-a` used	Expression to split by default is white space
`-i`	extension	Replace original file with results	Useful for modifying contents of files
`-I`	directory	Specify location of `include` files	
`-l`	octal character code	Drop newlines when used	With `-n` and `-p` and use designated character as line-termination character
`-n`	none	Process the script using each specified file as an argument	Used for performing the same set of actions on a set of files
`-p`	none	Same as `-n` but each line is printed	
`-P`	none	Run the script through the C preprocessor before Perl compiles it	

continues

Table 1 Continued

Option	Arguments	Purpose	Notes
`-s`	none	Enable passing of arbitrary switches to Perl	Use `-s -what -ever` to have the Perl variables `$what` and `$ever` defined within your script
`-S`	none	Tell Perl to look along the path for the script	
`-T`	none	Use taint checking; don't evaluate expressions supplied on the command line	
`-u`	none	Make Perl dump core after compiling your script; intended to allow for generation of Perl executables	Very messy; wait for the Perl compiler
`-U`	none	Unsafe mode; overrides Perl's natural caution	Don't use this!
`-v`	none	Print Perl version number	
`-w`	none	Print warnings about script syntax	Extremely useful, especially during development

TIP The `-e` option is handy for quick Perl operations from the command line. Want to change all instances of "oldstring" in Wiffle.bat to "newstrong"? Try

```
perl -i.old -p -e "s/ oldstring/ newstrong/g"
wiffle.bat
```

This says: "Take each line of `Wiffle.bat` (`-p`); store the original in `Wiffle.old` (`-i`); substitute all instances of `oldstring` with `newstrong` (`-e`); write the result (`-p`) to the original file (`-i`)."

You can supply Perl command-line arguments on the interpreter invocation line in UNIX scripts. The following line is a good start to any Perl script:

```
#!/usr/local/bin/perl -w -t
```

Table 2 shows the debug flags, which can be specified with the `-D` command-line option. If you specify a number, you can simply add all the numbers of each flag together so that 6 is 4 and 2. If you use the letter as a flag then simply list all the options required. The following two calls are equivalent:

```
#perl -d -D6 test.pl
#perl -d -Dls test.pl
```

Table 2 Perl Debugging Flags

Flag Number	Flag Letter	Meaning of Flag
1	p	Tokenizing and parsing
2	s	Stack snapshots
4	l	Label stack processing
8	t	Trace execution
16	o	Operator node construction
32	c	String/numeric conversions
64	P	Print preprocessor command for `-P`
128	m	Memory allocation
256	f	Format processing
512	r	Regular expression parsing
1024	x	Syntax tree dump
2048	u	Tainting checks
4096	L	Memory leaks (not supported anymore)
8192	H	Hash dump; usurps `values()`
6384	X	Scratchpad allocation (Perl 5 only)
32768	D	Cleaning up (Perl 5 only)

A Perl Script

A Perl program consists of an ordinary text file containing a series of Perl commands. Commands are written in what looks like a bastardized amalgam of C, shell script, and English. In fact, that's pretty much what it is.

Perl code can be quite free-flowing. The broad syntactic rules governing where a statement starts and ends are

- Leading white space is ignored. You can start a Perl statement anywhere you want: at the beginning of the line, indented for clarity (recommended), or even right-justified (definitely frowned on) if you like.
- Commands are terminated with a semicolon.
- White space outside of string literals is irrelevant; one space is as good as a hundred. That means you can split statements over several lines for clarity.
- Anything after a pound sign (#) is ignored. Use this to pepper your code with useful comments.

Here's a Perl statement inspired by Kurt Vonnegut:

```
print "My name is Yon Yonson\n";
```

No prizes for guessing what happens when Perl runs this code; it prints

```
My name is Yon Yonson
```

If the `\n` doesn't look familiar, don't worry; it simply means that Perl should print a newline character after the text; in other words, Perl should go to the start of the next line.

Printing more text is a matter of either stringing together statements or giving multiple arguments to the `print` function:

```
print "My name is Yon Yonson,\n";
print "I live in Wisconsin,\n",
      "I work in a lumbermill there.\n";
```

That's right, `print` is a function. It may not look like it in any of the examples so far, where there are no parentheses to delimit the function arguments, but it is a function, and it takes arguments. You can use parentheses in Perl functions if you like; it sometimes helps to make an argument list clearer. More accurately, in this example the function takes a single argument consisting of an arbitrarily long list. We'll have much more to say about lists and arrays later, in the "Data Types" section. There will be a few more examples of the more common functions in the remainder of this chapter, but refer to the "Functions" chapter for a complete run-down on all of Perl's built-in functions.

So what does a complete Perl program look like? Here's a trivial UNIX example, complete with the invocation line at the top and a few comments:

```
#!/usr/local/bin/perl -w                # Show warn-
                                        ings
print "My name is Yon Yonson,\n";      #
                                        Let'sintroduce

                                        ourselves
print "I live in Wisconsin,\n",
   "I work in a lumbermill there.\n"; # Remember
                                        the line
                                        breaks
```

That's not at all typical of a Perl program though; it's just a linear sequence of commands with no structural complexity. The "Flow Control" section later in this overview introduces some of the constructs that make Perl what it is. For now, we'll stick to simple examples like the preceding for the sake of clarity.

Data Types

Perl has a small number of data types. If you're used to working with C, where even characters can be either signed or unsigned, this makes a pleasant change. In essence, there are only two data types: *scalars* and *arrays*. There is also a very special kind of array called an *associative array* that merits a section all to itself.

Scalars

All numbers and strings are scalars. Scalar variable names start with a dollar sign.

NOTE All Perl variable names, including scalars, are case sensitive. `$Name` and `$name`, for example, are two completely different quantities.

Perl converts automatically between numbers and strings as required, so that

```
$a = 2;
$b = 6;
$c = $a . $b;  # The "." operator concatenates two
                 #strings
$d = $c / 2;
print $d;
```

yields the result

```
13
```

This example involves converting two integers into strings, concatenating the strings into a new string variable, converting this new string to an integer, dividing it by two, converting the result to a string, and printing it. All of these conversions are handled implicitly, leaving the programmer free to concentrate on what needs to be done rather than the low-level details of how it is to be done.

This might be a problem if Perl were regularly used for tasks where, for example, explicit memory offsets were used and data types were critical. But for the type of task where Perl is normally used, these automatic conversions are smooth, intuitive, and useful.

We can use this to develop the earlier example script using some string variables:

```
#!/usr/local/bin/perl -w          # Show warnings

$who = 'Yon Yonson';
$where = 'Wisconsin';
$what = 'in a lumbermill';

print "My name is $who,\n";     # Let's introduce
                                  ourselves
```

```
print "I live in $where,\n",
      "I work $what there.\n";        # Remember the
                                      line breaks

print "\nSigned: \t$who,\n\t\t$where.\n";
```

which yields

```
My name is Yon Yonson,
I work in Wisconsin,
I work in a lumbermill there.

Signed:    Yon Yonson,
     Wisconsin.
```

Arrays

A collection of scalars is an array. An array variable name starts with an @ sign, while an explicit array of scalars is written as a comma-separated list within parentheses:

```
@trees = ("Larch", "Hazel", "Oak");
```

Array subscripts are denoted using square brackets: `$trees[0]` is the first element of the `@trees` array. Notice that it's `@trees` but `$trees[0]`; individual array elements are scalars, so they start with a `$`.

Mixing scalar types in an array is not a problem. For example,

```
@items = (15, 45.67, "case");
print "Take $items[0] $items[2]s at \$$items[1]
each.\n";
```

results in

```
Take 15 cases at $45.67 each.
```

All arrays in Perl are dynamic. You never have to worry about memory allocation and management because Perl does all that stuff for you. Combine that with the fact that arrays can contain arrays as sub-arrays, and you're free to say things like the following:

```
@A = (1, 2, 3);
@B = (4, 5, 6);
@C = (7, 8, 9);
@D = (@A, @B, @C);
```

which results in the array `@D` containing numbers `1` through `9`. The power of constructs such as

```
@Annual = (@Spring, @Summer, @Fall, @Winter);
```

takes some getting used to.

NOTE An aspect of Perl that often confuses newcomers (and occasionally the old hands too) is the context-sensitive nature of evaluations. Perl keeps track of the context in which an expression is being evaluated and can return a different value in an array context than in a scalar context. In the following example

```
@A = (1, 2, 3, 4);
@B = @A;
$C = @A;
```

The array @B contains 1 through 4 while $C contains "4", the number of values in the array. Thiscontext-sensitivity becomes more of an issue when you use functions and operators that can take either a single argument or multiple arguments. The results can be quite different depending on what is passed to them.

Many of Perl's built-in functions take arrays as arguments. One example is `sort`, which takes an array as an argument and returns the same array sorted alphabetically:

```
print sort ( 'Beta', 'Gamma', 'Alpha' );
```

prints `AlphaBetaGamma`.

We can make this neater using another built-in function, `join`. This function takes two arguments: a string to connect with and an array of strings to connect. It returns a single string consisting of all elements in the array joined with the connecting string. For example,

```
print join ( ' : ', 'Name', 'Address', 'Phone'  );
```

returns the string `Name : Address : Phone`.

Since `sort` returns an array, we can feed its output straight into `join`:

```
print join( ', ', sort ( 'Beta', 'Gamma', 'Alpha' )
     );
```

prints `Alpha, Beta, Gamma.`

Note that we haven't separated the initial scalar argument of join from the array that follows it: The first argument is the string to join things with; the rest of the arguments are treated as a single argument, the array to be joined. This is true even if we use parentheses to separate groups of arguments:

```
print join( ': ', ('A', 'B', 'C'), ('D', 'E'),
     ('F', 'G', 'H', 'I'));
```

returns `A: B: C: D: E: F: G: H: I`. That's because of the way Perl treats arrays; adding an array to an array gives us one larger array, not two arrays. In this case, all three arrays get bundled into one.

TIP For even more powerful string-manipulation capabilities, refer to the `splice` function in "Functions" chapter.

Associative Arrays

There is a certain elegance to associative arrays that makes experienced Perl programmers a little snobbish about their language of choice. Rightly so! Associative arrays give Perl a degree of database functionality at a very low yet useful level. Many tasks that would otherwise involve complex programming can be reduced to a handful of Perl statements using associative arrays.

Arrays of the type we've already seen are *lists of values indexed by subscripts*. In other words, to get an individual element of an array, you supply a subscript as a reference:

```
@fruit = ("Apple", "Orange", "Banana");
```

```
print $fruit[2];
```

This example yields `Banana` because subscripts start at `0`, so `2` is the subscript for the third element of the `@fruit` array. A reference to

`$fruit[7]` here returns the null value, as no array element with that subscript has been defined.

Now, here's the point of all this: associative arrays are lists of values indexed by strings. Conceptually, that's all there is to them. Their implementation is more complex, obviously, as all of the strings need to be stored in addition to the values to which they refer.

When you want to refer to an element of an associative array, you supply a string (also called the *key*) instead of an integer (also called the subscript). Perl returns the corresponding value. Consider the following example:

```
%fruit = ("Green", "Apple", "Orange", "Orange",
      "Yellow", "Banana");

print $fruit{"Yellow"};
```

This prints `Banana` as before. The first line defines the associative array in much the same way as we have already defined ordinary arrays; the difference is that instead of listing values, we list *key/value pairs*. The first value is `Apple` and its key is `Green`; the second value is `Orange`, which happens to have the same string for both value and key; and the final value is `Banana` and its key is `Yellow`.

On a superficial level, this can be used to provide mnemonics for array references, allowing us to refer to `$Total{'June'}` instead of `$Total[5]`. But that's not even beginning to use the power of associative arrays. Think of the keys of an associative array as you might think of a key linking tables in a relational database, and you're closer to the idea:

```
%Folk =    ( 'YY', 'Yon Yonson',
             'TC', 'Terra Cotta',
             'RE', 'Ron Everly' );

%State = ( 'YY', 'Wisconsin',
           'TC', 'Minnesota',
           'RE', 'Bliss' );

%Job = ( 'YY', 'work in a lumbermill',
         'TC', 'teach nuclear physics',
         'RE', 'watch football');
```

```
foreach $person ( 'TS', 'YY', 'RE' )  {
        print "My name is $Folk{$person},\n",
              "I live in $State{$person},\n",
              "I $Job{$person} there.\n\n";
        }
```

The `foreach` construct is explained later in the "Flow Control" section; for now, you just need to know that it makes Perl execute the three `print` statements for each of the people in the list after the `foreach` keyword.

The keys and values of an associative array may be treated as separate (ordinary) arrays as well, by using the `keys` and `values` keywords respectively. For example,

```
print keys %Folk;
print values %State;
```

prints the string `YYRETCWisconsinBlissMinnesota`. String handling will be discussed later in this chapter.

NOTE There is a special associative array, `%ENV`, that stores the contents of all environment variables, indexed by variable name. So `$ENV{'PATH'}` returns the current search path, for example. Here's a way to print the current value of all environment variables, sorted by variable name for good measure:

```
foreach $var (sort keys %ENV ) {
     print "$var: \"$ENV{$var}\".\n";
     }
```

NOTE The `foreach` clause sets `$var` to each of the environment variable names in turn (in alphabetical order), and the `print` statement prints each name and value. As the symbol " is used to specify the beginning and end of the string being printed, when we actually want to print a " we have to tell Perl to ignore the special meaning of the character. This is done by prefixing it with a backslash character (this is sometimes called *quoting* a character).

File Handles

We'll finish our look at Perl data types with a look at file handles. Really this is not a data type but a special kind of literal string. A file handle behaves in many ways like a variable, however, so this is a good time to cover them. Besides, you won't get very far in Perl without them.

A file handle can be regarded as a pointer to a file from which Perl is to read or to which it will write. C programmers will be familiar with the concept. The basic idea is that you associate a handle with a file or device and then refer to the handle in the code whenever you need to perform a read or write operation.

File handles are generally written in all uppercase. Perl has some useful predefined file handles, which are listed in table 3.

Table 3 Perl's Predefined File Handles

File Handle	Points To
STDIN	Standard input, normally the keyboard.
STDOUT	Standard output, normally the console.
STDERR	Device where error messages should be written, normally the console.

The `print` statement can take a file handle as its first argument:

```
print STDERR "Oops, something broke.\n";
```

Note that there is no comma after the file handle, which helps Perl to figure out that the `STDERR` is not something to be printed. If you're uneasy with this implicit list syntax, you can put parentheses around all of the `print` arguments:

```
print (STDERR "Oops, something broke.\n");
```

Note that there is still no comma after the file handle.

TIP Use the standard file handles explicitly, especially in complex programs. It is sometimes convenient to redefine the standard input or output device for a while; make sure that you don't accidentally wind up writing to a file what should have gone to the screen.

The `open` function may be used to associate a new file handle with a file:

```
open (INDATA, "/etc/stuff/Friday.dat");
open (LOGFILE, ">/etc/logs/reclaim.log");
print LOGFILE "Log of reclaim procedure\n";
```

By default, `open` opens files for reading only. If you want to override this default behavior, add one of the special direction symbols from table 4 to the file name. That's what the > at the start of the file name in the second `output` statement is for; it tells Perl that we intend to write to the named file.

Table 4 Perl File Access Symbols

Symbol	Meaning
<	Opens the file for reading. This is the default action.
>	Opens the file for writing.
>>	Opens the file for appending.
+<	Opens the file for both reading and writing.
+>	Opens the file for both reading and writing.
| (before file name)	Treat file as command into which Perl is to pipe text.
| (after file name)	Treat file as command from which input is to be piped to Perl.

To take a more complex example, the following is one way to feed output to the `mypr` printer on a UNIX system:

```
open (MYLPR, "|lpr -Pmypr");
print MYLPR "A line of output\n";
close MYLPR;
```

There is a special Perl operator for reading from files. It consists of two angle brackets around the file handle of the file from which we want to read, and it returns the next line or lines of input from the file or device, depending on whether the operator is used in a scalar or an array context. When no more input remains, the operator returns False.

For example, a construct like the following

```
while (<STDIN>) {
print;
}
```

simply echoes each line of input back to the console until the Ctrl and D keys are pressed. That's because the print function takes the current default argument here, the most recent line of input. Refer to the "Special Variables" chapter later for an explanation.

If the user types

```
A
Bb
Ccc
^D
```

then the screen will look like

```
A
A
Bb
Bb
Ccc
Ccc
^D
```

Note that in this case, <STDIN> is in a scalar context, so one line of standard input is returned at a time. Compare that with the following example:

```
print <STDIN>;
```

In this case, because print expects an array of arguments (it can be a single element array, but it's an array as far as print is concerned), the <> operator obligingly returns all the contents of STDIN as an array and print prints it. This means that nothing is written to the console until the user presses the Ctrl and D keys:

```
A
Bb
Ccc
^Z
A
Bb
Ccc
```

This script prints out the contents of the file .signature, double-spaced:

```
open (SIGFILE, ".signature");
while ( <SIGFILE> )  {
      print; print "\n";
      }
```

The first `print` has no arguments, so it takes the current default argument and prints it. The second has an argument, so it prints that instead. Perl's habit of using default arguments extends to the <> operator: if used with no file handle, it is assumed that <ARGV> is intended. This expands to each line in turn of each file listed on the command line.

If no files are listed on the command line, it is instead assumed that `STDIN` is intended. So for example,

```
while (<>) {
print "more.... ";
}
```

keeps printing `more....` as long as something other than Ctrl+D appears on standard input.

NOTE Perl 5 allows array elements to be references to any data type. This makes it possible to build arbitrary data structures of the kind used in C and other high-level languages, but with all the power of Perl; you can, for example, have an array of associative arrays.

Flow Control

The examples we've seen so far have been quite simple, with little or no logical structure beyond a linear sequence of steps. We managed to sneak in the occasional `while` and `foreach`. Perl has all of the flow control mechanisms you'd expect to find in a high-level language, and this section takes you through the basics of each.

Logical Operators

Let's start with two operators that are used like glue holding Perl programs together: the `||` (or) and `&&` (and) operators. They take two operands and return either True or False depending on the operands:

```
$Weekend = $Saturday || $Sunday;
```

If either `$Saturday` or `$Sunday` is True, then `$Weekend` is True.

```
$Solvent = ($income > 3) && ($debts < 10);
```

`$Solvent` is True only if `$income` is greater than `3` and `$debts` is less than `10`.

Now consider the logic of evaluating one of these expressions. It isn't always necessary to evaluate both operands of either a `&&` or a `||` operator. In the first example, if `$Saturday` is True, then we know `$Weekend` is True, regardless of whether `$Sunday` is also True.

This means that having evaluated the left side of an `||` expression as True, the righthand side will not be evaluated. Combine this with Perl's easy way with data types, and you can say things like the following:

```
$value > 10 || print "Oops, low value $value
...\n";
```

If `$value` is greater than `10`, the right side of the expression is never evaluated, so nothing is printed. If `$value` is not greater than `10`, Perl needs to evaluate the right side to decide whether the expression as a whole is True or False. That means it evaluates the `print` statement, printing the message like

```
Oops, low value 6...
```

Okay, it's a trick, but it's a very useful one.

Something analogous applies to the `&&` operator. In this case, if the left side of an expression is False, then the expression as a whole is False and so Perl will not evaluate the right side. This can be used to produce the same kind of effect as our `||` trick but with the opposite sense:

```
$value > 10 && print "OK, value is high enough...\n";
```

As with most Perl constructs, the real power of these tricks comes when you apply a little creative thinking. Remember that the left and right sides of these expressions can be any Perl expression; think of them as conjunctions in a sentence rather than as logical operators and you'll get a better feel for how to use them. Expressions such as

```
$length <= 80 || die "Line too long.\n";
$errorlevel > 3 && warn "Hmmm, strange error level
       ($errorlevel)...\n";
open ( LOGFILE, ">install.log") || &bust("Log
      file");
```

give a little of the flavor of creative Perl.

The `&bust` in that last line is a subroutine call, by the way. Refer to the "Subroutines" section later in this chapter for more information.

Conditional Expressions

The basic kind of flow control is a simple branch: A statement is either executed or not depending on whether a logical expression is True or False. This can be done by following the statement with a modifier and a logical expression:

```
open ( INFILE, "./missing.txt") if $missing;
```

The execution of the statement is contingent upon both the evaluation of the expression and the sense of the operator.

The expression evaluates as either True or False and can contain any of the relational operators listed in table 5, although it doesn't have to. Examples of valid expressions are

```
$full
$a == $b
<STDIN>
```

Table 5 Perl's Relational Operators

Operator	Numeric Context	String Context
Equality	`==`	`eq`
Inequality	`!=`	`ne`
Inequality with signed result	`<=>`	`cmp`
Greater than	`>`	`gt`
Greater than or equal to	`>=`	`ge`
Less than	`<`	`lt`
Less than or equal to	`<=`	le

NOTE What exactly does "less than" mean when we're comparing strings? It means "lexically less than." If `$left` comes before `$right` when the two are sorted alphabetically, `$left` is less than `$right`.

There are four modifiers, each of which behaves the way you might expect from the corresponding English word:

- `if` The statement executes if the logical expression is True and does not execute otherwise. Examples:

```
$max = 100 if $min < 100;
```

```
print "Empty!\n" if !$full;
```

- `unless` The statement does not execute if the logical expression is True and executes otherwise. Examples:

```
open (ERRLOG, "test.log") unless $NoLog;
print "Success" unless $error>2;
```

- `while` The statement executes repeatedly until the logical expression is False. Examples:

```
$total -= $decrement while $total > $decrement;
$n=1000;  "print $n\n" while $n— > 0;
```

- `until` Thestatement executes repeatedly until the logical expression is True. Examples:

```
$total += $value[$count++] until $total > $limit;
print RESULTS "Next value: $value[$n++]" until
    $value[$n] = -1;
```

Note that the logical expression is evaluated once only in the case of `if` and `unless` but multiple times in the case of `while` and `until`. In other words, the first two are simple conditionals, while the last two are loop constructs.

Compound Statements

The syntax changes when we want to make the execution of multiple statements contingent on the evaluation of a logical expression. The modifier comes at the start of a line, followed by the logical expression in parentheses, followed by the conditional statements contained in braces. Note that the parentheses around the logical expression are required, unlike with the single statement branching described in the previous section. For example,

```
if ( ( $total += $value ) > $limit )  {
   print LOGFILE "Maximum limit $limit exceeded.",
   " Offending value was $value.\n";
close (LOGFILE);
  die "Too many! Check the log file for
```

```
details.\n";
   }
```

This is somewhat similar to C's `if` syntax, except that the braces around the conditional statement block are required rather than optional.

The `if` statement is capable of a little more complexity, with `else` and `elseif` operators:

```
if ( !open( LOGFILE, "install.log") )   {
   close ( INFILE );
   die "Unable to open log file!\n";
   }
elseif ( !open( CFGFILE, ">system.cfg") )  {
   print LOGFILE "Error during install:",
   " Unable to open config file for writing.\n";
close ( LOGFILE );
   die "Unable to open config file for writing!\n";
   }
else  {
   print CFGFILE "Your settings go here!\n";
   }
```

Loops

The loopmodifiers (`while`, `until`, `for`, and `foreach`) are used with compound statements in much the same way:

```
until ( $total >= 50 )  {
   print "Enter a value: ";
   $value = scalar (<STDIN>);
   $total += $value;
   print "Current total is $total\n";
   }
print "Enough!\n";
```

The `while` and `until` statements were described in the earlier "Conditional Expressions" section. The `for` statement resembles the one in

C: It is followed by an initial value, a termination condition, and an iteration expression, all enclosed in parentheses and separated by semicolons:

```
for ( $count = 0; $count < 100; $count++ )   {
   print "Something";
   }
```

The `foreach` operator is special. It iterates over the contents of an array and executes the statements in a statement block for each element of the array. A simple example is the following:

```
@numbers = ("one", "two", "three", "four");
foreach $num ( @numbers )    {
   print "Number $num...\n";
   }
```

The variable `$num` first takes on the value `one`, then `two`, and so on. That example looks fairly trivial, but the real power of this operator lies in the fact that it can operate on any array:

```
foreach $arg ( @ARGV )    {
   print "Argument: \"$arg\".\n";
   }

foreach $namekey ( sort keys %surnames )   {
   print REPORT "Surname: $value{$namekey}.\n",
                "Address: $address{$namekey}.\n";
   }
```

Labels

Labels may be used with the `next`, `last`, and `redo` statements to provide more control over program flow through loops. A label consists of any word, usually in uppercase, followed by a colon. The label appears just before the loop operator (`while`, `for`, or `foreach`) and can be used as an anchor for jumping to from within the block:

```
RECORD:  while ( <INFILE> )   {
   $even = !$even;
   next RECORD if $even;
   print;
   }
```

That code snippet prints all the odd-numbered records in `INFILE`.

The three label control statements are

- `next` Jumps to the next iteration of the loop marked by the label or to the innermost enclosing loop if no label is specified.
- `last` Immediately breaks out of the loop marked by the label or out of the innermost enclosing loop if no label is specified.
- `redo` Jumps back to the loop marked by the specified label or to the innermost enclosing loop if no label is specified. This causes the loop to execute again with the same iterator value.

Subroutines

The basicsubunit of code in Perl is a subroutine. This is similar to a function in C and a procedure or a function in Pascal. A subroutine may be called with various parameters and returns a value. Effectively, the subroutine groups together a sequence of statements so that they can be re-used.

The Simplest Form of Subroutine

Subroutines can be declared anywhere in a program. If more than one subroutine with the same name is declared each new version replaces the older ones so that only the last one is effective. It is possible to declare subroutines within an `eval()` expression, these will not actually be declared until the runtime execution reaches the `eval()` statement.

Subroutines are declared using the following syntax:

```
sub subroutine-name {
                statements
}
```

The simplest form of subroutine is one that does not return any value and does not access any external values. The subroutine is called by prefixing the name with the & character. (There are other ways of calling subroutines, which are explained in more detail later.) An example of a program using the simplest form of subroutine illustrates this:

```
#!/usr/bin/perl -w
# Example of subroutine which does not use
# external values and does not return a value
&egsub1; # Call the subroutine once
&egsub1; # Call the subroutine a second time
sub egsub1 {
     print "This subroutine simply prints this
     line.\n";
}
```

TIP While it is possible to refer from a subroutine to any global variable directly, it is normally considered bad programming practice. Reference to global variables from subroutines makes it more difficult to re-use the subroutine code. It is best to make any such references to external values explicit by passing explicit parameters to the subroutine as described in the following section. Similarly it is best to avoid programming subroutines that directly change the values of global variables because doing so can lead to unpredictable side-effects if the subroutine is re-used in a different program. Use explicit return values or explicit parameters passed by reference as described in the following section.

Returning Values from Subroutines

Subroutines can also return values, thus acting as functions. The return value is the value of the last statement executed. This can be a scalar or an array value.

CAUTION Take care not to add seemingly innocuous statements near the end of a subroutine. A `print` statement returns `1`, for example, so a subroutine which prints just before it returns will always return `1`.

It is possible to test whether the calling context requires an array or a scalar value using the `wantarray` construct, thus returning different values depending on the required context. For example,

```
wantarray ? (a, b, c) : 0;
```

as the last line of a subroutine returns the array `(a, b, c)` in an array context, and the scalar value `0` in a scalar context.

```
#!/usr/bin/perl -w
# Example of subroutine which does not use
# external values but does return a value
# Call the subroutine once, returning a scalar
  #value
$scalar-return = &egsub2;
print "Scalar return value: $scalar-return.\n";
# Call the subroutine a second time, returning an
  #array value
@array-return = &egsub2;
print "Array return value:", @array-return, ".\n";
sub egsub2 {
     print "This subroutine prints this line and
returns a value.\n";
     wantarray ? (a, b, c) : 0;
}
```

It is possible to return from a subroutine before the last statement by using the `return()` function. The argument to the `return()` function is the returned value in this case. This is illustrated in the following example, which is not a very efficient way to do the test but illustrates the point:

```
#!/usr/bin/perl -w
# Example of subroutine which does not use
# external values but does return a value using
  #"return"
$returnval = &egsub3; # Call the subroutine once
print "The current time is $returnval.\n";
sub egsub3 {
     print "This subroutine prints this line and
       returns a value.\n";
     local($sec, $min, $hour, @rest) =
          gmtime(time);
     ($min == 0) && ($hour == 12) && (return
```

```
        "noon");
    if ($hour > 12)
        return "after noon";
    else
        return "before noon";
}
```

Note that it is usual to make any variables used within a subroutine `local()` to the enclosing block. This means that they will not interfere with any variables that have the same name in the calling program. In Perl 5, these may be made lexically local rather than dynamically local, using `my()` instead of `local()` (this is discussed in more detail later).

When returning multiple arrays, the result is flattened into one list so that, effectively, only one array is returned. So in the following example all the return values are in `@return-a1` and the send array `@return-a2` is empty.

```
#!/usr/bin/perl -w
# Example of subroutine which does not use
# external values returning an array
 (@return-a1, @return-a2) = &egsub4; # Call the
subroutine once
print "Return array a1",@return-a1,
   " Return array a2 ",@return-a2, ".\n";
sub egsub4 {
    print "This subroutine returns a1 and a2.\n";
    local(@a1) = (a, b, c);
    local(@a2) = (d, e, f);
    return(@a1,@a2);
}
```

In Perl 4, this problem can be avoided by passing the arrays by reference using a `typeglob` (see the following section). In Perl 5, you can do this and also manipulate any variable by reference directly (see the following section).

Passing Values to Subroutines

The next important aspect of subroutines, is that the call can pass values to the subroutine. The call simply lists the variables to be passed, and these are passed in the list @_ to the subroutine. These are known as the parameters or the arguments. It is customary to assign each value a name at the start of the subroutine so that it is clear what is going on. Manipulation of these copies of the arguments is equivalent to passing arguments by value (that is, their values may be altered but this does not alter the value of the variable in the calling program).

```
#!/usr/bin/perl -w
# Example of subroutine is passed external values
  by #value
$returnval = &egsub5(45,3); # Call the subroutine
once
print "The (45+1) * (3+1) is $returnval.\n";
$x = 45;
$y = 3;
$returnval = &egsub5($x,$y);
print "The ($x+1) * ($y+1) is $returnval.\n";
print "Note that \$x still is $x, and \$y still is
$y.\n";
sub egsub5 { # Access $x and $y by value
    local($x, $y) = @_;
    return ($x++ * $y++);
}
```

To pass scalar values by reference, rather than by value, the elements in @_ can be accessed directly. This will change their values in the calling program. In such a case, the argument must be a variable rather than a literal value, as literal values cannot be altered.

```
#!/usr/bin/perl -w
# Example of subroutine is passed external values
by #reference
$x = 45;
$y = 3;
print "The ($x+1) * ($y+1) ";
$returnval = &egsub6($x,$y);
```

```
print "is $returnval.\n";
print "Note that \$x now is $x, and \$y now is
     $y.\n";
sub egsub6 { # Access $x and $y by reference
     return ($_[0]++ * $_[0]++);
}
```

Array values can be passed by reference in the same way. However several restrictions apply. First, as with returned array values, the `@_` list is one single flat array, so passing multiple arrays this way is tricky. Also, although individual elements may be altered in the subroutine using this method, the size of the array cannot be altered within the subroutine (so `push()` and `pop()` cannot be used).

Therefore, another method has been provided to facilitate the passing of arrays by reference. This method is known as *typeglobbing* and works with Perl 4 or Perl 5. The principle is that the subroutine declares that one or more of its parameters are typeglobbed, which means that all the references to that identifier in the scope of the subroutine are taken to refer to the equivalent identifier in the namespace of the calling program. The syntax for this declaration is to prefix the identifier with an asterisk, rather than an @ sign, this `*array1` typeglobs `@array1`. In fact, typeglobbing links all forms of the identifier so the `*array1` typeglobs `@array1`, `%array1`, and `$array1` (any reference to any of these in the local subroutine actually refers to the equivalent variable in the calling program's namespace). It only makes sense to use this construct within a `local()` list, effectively creating a local alias for a set of global variables. So the previous example becomes the following:

```
#!/usr/bin/perl -w
# Example of subroutine using arrays passed by
  #reference (typeglobbing)
&egsub7(@a1,@a2); # Call the subroutine once
print "Modified array a1",@a1," Modified array a2
     ",@a2, ".\n";
sub egsub7 {
     local(*a1,*a2) = @_;
     print "This subroutine modifies a1 and a2.\n";
```

```
    @a1 = (a, b, c);
    @a2 = (d, e, f);
}
```

In Perl 4, this is the only way to use references to variables, rather than variables themselves. In Perl 5, there is also a generalized method for dealing with references. Although this method looks more awkward in its syntax because of the abundance of underscores, it is actually more precise in its meaning. Typeglobbing automatically aliases the scalar, the array, and the hashed array form of an identifier, even if only the array name is required. With Perl 5 references, this distinction can be made explicit; only the array form of the identifier is referenced.

```
#!/usr/bin/perl -w
# Example of subroutine using arrays passed
# by reference (Perl 5 references)
&egsub7(\@a1,\@a2); # Call the subroutine once
print "Modified array a1",@a1," Modified array a2
     ",@a2, ".\n";
sub egsub7 {
    local($a1ref,$a2ref) = @_;
    print "This subroutine modifies a1 and a2.\n";
    @$a1ref = (a, b, c);
    @$a2ref = (d, e, f);
}
```

Subroutine Recursion

One the most powerful features of subroutines is their ability to call themselves. There are many problems that can be solved by repeated application of the same procedure. However, care must be taken to set up a termination condition where the recursion stops and the execution can unravel itself. Typical examples of this approach are found when processing lists: Process the head item and then process the tail; if the tail is empty do not recurse. Another neat example is the calculation of a factorial value:

```
#!/usr/bin/perl -w
#
# Example factorial using recursion
```

```
for ($x=1; $x<100; $x++) {
        print "Factorial $x is ",&factorial($x),
              "\n";
}

sub factorial {
        local($x) = @_;
        if ($x == 1) {
                return 1;
        }
        else {
                return ($x*($x-1) + &factorial($x-
1));
        }
}
```

Issues of Scope with *my()* and *local()*

Issues of scope are very important with relation to subroutines. In particular all variables inside subroutines should be made lexical local variables (using `my()`) or dynamic local variables (using `local()`). In Perl 4, the only choice is `local()` because `my()` was only introduced in Perl 5.

Variables declared using the `my()` construct are considered to be lexical local variables. They are not entered in the symbol table for the current package. Therefore, they are totally hidden from all contexts other than the local block within which they are declared. Even subroutines called from the current block cannot access lexical local variables in that block. Lexical local variables must begin with an alphanumeric character or an underscore.

Variables declared using the `local()` construct are considered to be dynamic local variables. The value is local to the current block and any calls from that block. It is possible to localize special variables as dynamic local variables, but these cannot be made into lexical local variables. The following two differences from lexical local variables show the two cases in Perl 5 where it is still advisable to use `local()` rather than `my()`:

- Use `local()` if you want the value of the local variables to be visible to subroutines
- Use `local()` if you are localizing special variables

Pattern Matching

We'll finish this overview of Perl with a look at Perl's pattern matching capabilities. The ability to match and replace patterns is vital to any scripting language that claims to be capable of useful text manipulation. By this stage, you probably won't be surprised to read that Perl matches patterns better than any other general purpose language. Perl 4's patterns matching was excellent, but Perl 5 has introduced some significant improvements, including the ability to match even more arbitrary strings than before.

The basic pattern matching operations we'll be looking at are

- Matching   Where we want to know of a particular string matches a pattern
- Substitution   Where we want to replace portions of a string based on a pattern

The patterns referred to here are more properly known as *regular expressions*, and we'll start by looking at them.

Regular Expressions

A regular expression is a set of rules describing a generalized string. If the characters that make up a particular string conform to the rules of a particular regular expression, then the regular expression is said to match that string.

A few concrete examples usually helps after an overblown definition like that. The regular expression `b.` will match the strings `bovine`, `above`, `Bobby`, and `Bob Jones` but not the strings `Bell`, `b`, or `Bob`. That's because the expression insists that the letter `b` must be in the string and it must be followed immediately by another character.

The regular expression b+, on the other hand, requires the lowercase letter b at least once. This matches b and Bob in addition to the example matches for b.. The regular expression b* requires zero or more bs, so it will match any string. That is fairly useless, but it makes more sense as part of a larger regular expression; for example, Bob*y matches Boy, Boby, and Bobby but not Boboby.

Assertions

There are a number of so-called *assertions* that are used to anchor parts of the pattern to word or string boundaries. The ^ assertion matches the start of a string, so the regular expression ^fool matches fool and foolhardy but not tomfoolery or April fool. The assertions are listed in table 6.

Table 6 Perl's Regular Expression Assertions

Assertion	Matches	Example	Matches	Doesn't Match
^	Start of string	^fool	foolish	tomfoolery
$	End of string	fool$	April fool	foolish
\b	Word boundary	be\bside	be side	beside
\B	Non-word boundary	be\Bside	beside	be side

Atoms

The . we saw in b. is an example of a regular expression *atom*. Atoms are, as the name suggests, the fundamental building blocks of a regular expression. A full list appears in table 7.

Table 7 Perl's Regular Expression Atoms

Atom	Matches	Example	Matches	Doesn't Match
.	Any character except newline	`b.b`	`bob`	`bb`
List of characters in square brackets	Any one of those characters	`^[Bb]`	`Bob`, `bob`	`Rbob`
Regular expression in parentheses	Anything that regular expression matches	`^a(b.b)c$`	`abobc`	`abbc`

Quantifiers

A *quantifier* is a modifier for an atom. It can be used to specify that a particular atom must appear at least once, for example, as in `b+`. The atom quantifiers are listed in table 8.

Table 8 Perl's Regular Expression Atom Quantifiers

Quantifier	Matches	Example	Matches	Doesn't Match
*	Zero or more instances of the atom	`ab*c`	`ac`, `abc`	`abb`
+	One or more instances of the atom	`ab+c`	`abc`	`ac`
?	Zero or one instances of the atom	`ab?c`	`ac`, `abc`	`abbc`
{*n*}	*n* instances of the atom	`ab{2}c`	`abbc`	`abbbc`
{*n*,}	At least *n* instances of the atom	`ab{2,}c`	`abbc`, . `abbbc`	`abc`

continues

Quantifier	Matches	Example	Matches	Doesn't Match
`{nm}`	At least *n*, at most *m* instances of the atom	`ab{2,3}c`	`abbc`	`abbbbc`

Special Characters

There are a number of special characters denoted by the backslash; `\n` being especially familiar to C programmers perhaps. Table 9 lists the special characters.

Table 9 Perl Regular Expression's Special Characters

Symbol	Matches	Example	Matches	Doesn't Match
`\d`	Any digit	`b\dd`	`b4d`	`bad`
`\D`	Non-digit	`b\Dd`	`bdd`	`b4d`
`\n`	Newline			
`\r`	Carriage return			
`\t`	Tab			
`\f`	Formfeed			
`\s`	White space character			
`\S`	Non-white space character			
`\w`	Alphanumeric character		`a\wb`	`a2b a^b`
`\W`	Non-alphanumeric character		`a\Wb`	`aa^b aabb`

Backslashed Tokens

It is essential that regular expressions are able to use all characters so that all possible strings occuring in the real word can be matched. With so many characters having special meanings, a mechanism is therefore required that allows us to represent any arbitrary character in a regular expression.

This is done using a backslash followed by a numeric quantity. This quantity can take on any of the following formats:

- Single or double digit Matched quantities after a match. These are called *backreferences* and will be explained in the later "Matching" section.
- Two or three digit octal number The character with that number as character code, unless it's possible to interpret it as a backreference.
- `x` followed by two hexadecimal digits The character with that number as its character code. For example, `\x3e` is >.
- `c` followed by a single character This is the control character. For example, `\cG` matches Ctrl+G.
- Any other character This is the character itself. For example, `\&` matches the `&` character.

Matching

Let's start putting all of that together with some real pattern matching. The match operator normally consists of two forward slashes with a regular expression in between, and it normally operates on the contents of the `$_` variable. So if `$_` is `serendipity`, then `/^ser/`, `/end/`, and `/^s.*y$/` are all True.

Matching on $_

The `$_` operator is special; it is described in full in "Special Variables" chapter in this book. In many ways, it is the default container for data being read in by Perl; the `<>` operator, for example, gets the next line from `STDIN` and stores it in `$_`. So the following code snippet lets you type lines of text and tells you when your line matches one of the regular expressions:

```
$prompt = "Enter some text or press Ctrl-Z to stop:
        ";
print $prompt;
while (<>)  {
   /^[aA]/ && print "Starts with a or A.  ";
   /[0-9]$/ && print "Ends with a digit.  ";
   /perl/ && print "You said it!   ";
   print $prompt;
   }
```

Bound Matches

Matching doesn't always have to operate on `$_`, although this default behavior is quite convenient. There is a special operator, `=~`, that evaluates to either True or False depending on whether its first operand matches on its second operand. For example, `$filename =~ /dat$/` is True if `$filename` matches on `/dat$/`. This can be used in conditionals in the usual way:

```
$filename =~ /dat$/ && die "Can't use .dat
     files.\n";
```

There is a corresponding operator with the opposite sense, `!~`. This is True if the first operator does not match the second:

```
$ENV{'PATH'} !~ /perl/ && warn "Not sure if perl is
     in your path...";
```

Alternate Delimiters

The match operator can use other characters instead of `//`; a useful point if you're trying to match a complex expression involving forward slashes. A more general form of the match operator than `//` is `m//`. If you use the leading `m` here, then any character may be used to delimit the regular expression. For example,

```
$installpath =~ m!^/usr/local!
    || warn "The path you have chosen is odd.\n";
```

Match Options

A number of optional switches may be applied to the match operator (either the `//` or `m//` forms) to alter its behavior. These options are listed in table 10.

Table 10 Perl Match Operator's Optional Switches

Switch	Meaning
g	Perform global matching
i	Case-insensitive matching
o	Evaluate the regular expression once only

The g switch continues matching even after the first match has been found. This is useful when using backreferences to examine the matched portions of a string, as described in the later "Backreferences" section.

The o switch is used inside loops where a lot of pattern matching is taking place. It tells Perl that the regular expression (the match operator's operand) is to be evaluated once only. This can improve efficiency in cases where the regular expression is fixed for all iterations of the loop that contains it.

Backreferences

As we mentioned earlier in the "Backslashed Tokens" section, pattern matching produces quantities known as backreferences. These are the parts of your string where the match succeeded. You need to tell Perl to store them by surrounding the relevant parts of your regular expression with parentheses, and they may be referred to after the match as \1, \2, and so on. In this example, we check if the user has typed three consecutive four-letter words:

```
while (<>)  {
   /\b(\S{4})\s(\S{4})\s(\S{4})\b/
   && print "Gosh, you said $1 $2 $3!\n";
}
```

The first four-letter word lies between a word boundary (\b) and some white space (\s) and consists of four non-white space characters (\S). If matched, the matching substring is stored in the special variable \1 and the search continues. Once the search is complete, the backreferences may be referred to as $1, $2, and so on.

What if you don't know in advance how many matches to expect? Perform the match in an array context, and Perl returns the matches in an array. Consider this example:

```
@hits = ("Yon Yonson, Wisconsin" =~ /(\won)/g);
print "Matched on ", join(', ', @hits), ".\n";
```

Let's start at the right side and work back. The regular expression (\won) means that we match any alphanumeric character followed by on and store all three characters. The g option after the // operator means that we want to do this for the entire string, even after we've found a match. The =~ operator means that we carry out this operation on a given string, `Yon Yonson, Wisconsin`; and finally, the whole thing is evaluated in an array context, so Perl returns the array of matches and we store it in the `@hits` array. The output from this example is

```
Matched on yon, Yon, son, con.
```

Substitution

Once you get the hang of pattern matching, substitutions are quite straightforward and very powerful. The substitution operator is `s///` that resembles the match operator but has three rather than two slashes. As with the match operator, any other character may be substituted for forward slashes, and the optional `i`, `g`, and `o` switches may be used.

The pattern to be replaced goes between the first and second delimiters, and the replacement pattern goes between the second and third. To take a simple example,

```
$house = "henhouse";
$house  =~ s/hen/dog/;
```

change `$house` from `henhouse` to `doghouse`. Note that it isn't possible to use the =~ operation with a literal string in the way we did when matching; that's because you can't modify a literal constant. Instead, store the string in a variable and modify that.

SPECIAL VARIABLES

This section looks in detail at the special variables used in Perl. Under standing these variables is crucial to programming effectively in Perl. Some of the variables are essential for nearly all Perl programs, while others are merely useful shortcuts that can avoid the need to run external programs that extract information from the system.

Each variable may have three possible names:

- Long name (or English name)
- Intermediate name
- Short name

Most existing Perl programs use only the short name form. This is unfortunate, as the short name is usually a cryptic symbol. The use of these symbols in Perl programs may be daunting at first, especially in complex expressions comprising multiple variables. However, with the aid of this chapter, it soon becomes easy to identify their meaning and, thus, understand the programs.

The long name was introduced in Perl 5. This chapter lists all the special variables of this *English* name, in alphabetical order. In Perl 4, you must use the short name. In Perl 5, you can use any of the name forms, but if you want to use the long English name, you must include the following command:

```
Use English;
```

This command enables the long names in the Perl 5 program.

Sometimes (in particular where the same variable also exists in awk, the UNIX report processor) an intermediate name is also allowed. Again this requires the use of the English module and is not available in Perl 4. This means that those who are used the awk conventions can use them if they wish.

This chapter categorizes special variables in several ways to make it easier for you to use the list as a reference source. The most important of these categories is Scope, which can have the following values:

- *always global* These variables are global but have an unambiguous context (they need not be made local in a subroutine).
- *localize* These variables are global and may need to be made local in subroutines if the value is being changed (especially to prevent unplanned subroutine side effects).

  local These variables are always local and do not need to be made local explicitly.

The other important special-variable category used in this chapter is File Handle Call. Special variables that implicitly refer to the current active file handle can be explicitly bound to any existing file handle. This facility must be activated by the following call:

```
use FileHandle;
```

This enables calls of the forms

```
FILEHANDLE->method(EXPR)
method FILEHANDLE EXPR
```

The relevant `method` name usually is the full long name of the special variable. The optional `EXPR` is an expression for changing the current value of the file handle, as well as referring to another file handle for the purposes of the special-variable reference. This syntax may seem confusing at first, but when used consistently, it can make Perl programs with formatting much more readable.

Both the English long names and the use of file handles in references to formats are new features in Perl 5. If you are using Perl 4, you must use the short names and allow format operations to take place in relation to the current active file handle, which you can change by using the `select()` function.

$<I<digit>>

Compliance

4 **5** **NT**

Syntax

Short Name `$1, $2, ... $<N>`
Scope `local` *(read-only)*

Definition

These variables are used to refer back to pattern matches. In any pattern to be matched, sets of parentheses are used to mark subpatterns. These subpatterns are numbered from left to right. After a match has been made, each subpattern match is referenced by these variables, up to and including the number of subpatterns that are actually specified. `$1` is the first subpattern, `$2` is the second, and so on, up to and including `$<N>`, the Nth subpattern specified.

All subpatterns after the last one (`$<N+1>`, for example), are equal to `undef`.

Example

```
$_ = "AlphaBetaGamma";
/^(Alpha)(.*)(Gamma)$/;
print "$1 then $2 then $3\n";
```

TIP If you have alternative patterns and do not know which one may have matched, try using `$LAST_PAREN_MATCH` instead.

$[$#

Compliance

$# index of the last cell

4 **5** **NT**

Syntax

Short Name `$[`

Scope `localize`

Definition

This variable, which is usually set to a value of 0, represents the index of the first element in any array. Programmers who are used to using 1 as the index of the first element of an array could change the value of this variable to suit their preference.

Example

```
$[ = 1;
$_ = "AlphaBetaGamma";
$tmp = index($_,"Beta");
print "Beta located at: $tmp\n";
$[ = 0;
$_ = "AlphaBetaGamma";
$tmp = index($_,"Beta");
print "Beta located at: $tmp\n";
```

$ACCUMULATOR

Compliance

5 **NT**

Syntax

Short Name `$^A`
Scope `always global`

Definition

This variable allows direct access to the line of output built up with the Perl formatting commands. Normally, this access is not necessary, but it is possible.

Example

```
$tmp = formline<<‘FINISH’, Alpha, Beta, Gamma;
@<<<<<<<<<<  @|||||||||||| @<<<<<<<<<
FINISH
print “Accumulator now contains:\n $^A\n”;
$^A = “”;
```

$ARG

Compliance

4 5 NT

Syntax

Short Name `$_`
Scope `localize`

Definition

This variable is the default pattern space. When reading a file, `$ARG` usually takes on the value of each line in turn. You can assign a value to `$ARG` directly. Many functions and operators take this variable as the default upon which to operate, so you can make the code more concise by using `$ARG`.

Example

```
$_ = "\$\_ is the default for many operations
including print().\n";
print;
```

$ARGV

Compliance

4 5 NT

Syntax

Short Name `$ARGV`
Scope `always global`

Definition

When processing an input file, this variable provides access to the name of this file.

Example

```
print("Assuming this script has been called with an
argument as a i/p file:_
 while (<>){
      print "$ARGV\n";
      };
```

$BASETIME

Compliance

4 5 NT

Syntax

Short Name `$^T`
Scope `localize`

Definition

This variable is the time when the Perl program was started, as measured in the basic time units (seconds since the start of 1970).

Example

```
$nicetime = localtime($^T);
print "This program started at $^T (i.e.
$nicetime).\n";
```

$CHILD_ERROR

Compliance

4 5 NT

Syntax

Short Name `$?`
Scope `localize`

Definition

If a Perl script spawns child processes, you can examine their error codes by using this variable.

Example

```
'ls -lgd /vir';
print "Child Process error was: $?\n";
```

$DEBUGGING

Compliance

4 5 NT

Syntax

Short Name `$^D`
Scope `localize`

Definition

Perl can be run in debugging mode. This variable allows the value of this flag to be accessed and altered.

NOTE Debugging is only allowed if the version of Perl you are using was compiled with DEBUGGING specifically set.

Example

```
print "The debug flags are: $^D\n";
```

$EFFECTIVE_GROUP_ID

Compliance

4 5 NT

Syntax

Short Name `$)`
Intermediate Name `$EGID`
Scope `localize`

Definition

In systems that support users and groups, as well as setting new users and groups within a process, Perl can access both the original and the effective user and group information. The effective group variable provides access to a list of numbers that represent the *effective group identifiers* (*GIDs*).

Example

```
print("Effective Group ID is a list of GIDs:
     $)\n");
```

$EFFECTIVE_USER_ID

Compliance

4 5 NT

Syntax

Short Name `$>`
Intermediate Name `$EUID`
Scope `localize`

Definition

In systems that support users and groups, as well as setting new users and groups within a process, Perl can access both the original and the effective user and group information. The effective user variable provides access to a single number that represents the *effective user identifier* (*UID*).

Example

```
print("Effective User ID is one UID: $>\n");
```

$EVAL_ERROR

Compliance

4 5 NT

Syntax

Short Name `$@`
Scope `localize`

Definition

Perl allows explicit calls to the `eval()` function to evaluate Perl syntax with a Perl script. This variable allows access to the returned error after such an operation. The error is a string that contains the relevant error message.

Example

```
print "Passing eval a malformed Perl
expression:\n";
eval 'print "Hello';
print "Error: $@\n";
```

$EXECUTABLE_NAME

Compliance

4 5 NT

Syntax

Short Name `$^X`
Scope `localize`

Definition

This variable provides access to the name of the Perl executable used by the script.

Example

```
print "Executable name of Perl is: $^X\n";
```

$FORMAT_FORMFEED

Compliance

5 NT

Syntax

Short Name `$^L`
Scope `always global`
File Handle Call `format_formfeed FILEHANDLE EXPR`

Definition

When you use the Perl formatting commands, you can specify formats to manipulate centering and other formatting of the text. One additional option is to specify the exact code to be inserted between pages of output in the file. The default value is a form-feed character (`\f`), but this can be changed.

Example

```
if ($^L = '\f')
{
  print "The formfeed character is the default
break between pages.\n";
}
```

$FORMAT_LINES_LEFT

Compliance

4 5 NT

Syntax

Short Name `$-`
Scope `always global`
File Handle Call `format_lines_left FILEHANDLE EXPR`

Definition

When you use the Perl formatting commands, this counter, which exists for each file handle with an associated format, is decremented every time a line is output until it reaches zero, when a new page is generated. You can manually set this variable to zero to force a page break in the output.

Example

```
format EG_FORMAT =
@<<<<<<<<<<  @||||||||||| @>>>>>>>>> ^||||||||||
$one,       $two,          $three     $fitme
.
open(EG_FORMAT,">-");
select(EG_FORMAT);
$one = 'Left';
$two = 'Center';
$three = 'Right';
$fitme= "";
write;
$one = $-;
$two = $-;
$three = $-;
write;
$one = $-;
$two = $-;
$three = $-;
```

```
write;
select(STDOUT);
```

$FORMAT_LINES_PER_PAGE

Compliance

4 5 NT

Syntax

Short Name `$=`
Scope `always global`
File Handle Call `format_lines_per_page FILEHANDLE EXPR`

Definition

Each format file handle has an associated number of lines per page, which you can access and change by using this variable.

Example

```
select(EG_FORMAT);
$one = 'Left';
$two = 'Center';
$three = 'Right';
$fitme= "";
write;
$one = $=;
$two = $=;
$three = $=;
write;
select(STDOUT);
```

$FORMAT_LINE_BREAK_CHARACTERS

Compliance

4 5 NT

Syntax

Short Name `$:`
Scope `localize`
File Handle Call `format_line_break_characters FILEHANDLE EXPR`

Definition

When you are outputting a value to a formatted area by using the format code

^||||||||||||||

(or the other multiple-line formats), the line-break character determines how strings are split into lines to fit into the formatted space. By default, the legal break characters are space, hyphen, and new line.

Example

```
select(EG_FORMAT);
$: = ' \n-';
$one = 1;
$two = 2;
$three = 3;
$fitme= "One-One-One-One-One-One";
write;
write;
write;
select(STDOUT);
```

$FORMAT_NAME

Compliance

4 5 NT

Syntax

Short Name `$~`
Scope `always global`
File Handle Call `format_name FILEHANDLE EXPR`

Definition

Each format has a name, which may also be the name of the file handle. You can access the name directly through this variable.

Example

```
select(EG_FORMAT);
$one = $~;
$two = $~;
$three = $~;
write;
select(STDOUT);
```

$FORMAT_PAGE_NUMBER

Compliance

4 5 NT

Syntax

Short Name `$%`
Scope `always global`
File Handle Call `format_page_number FILEHANDLE EXPR`

Definition

Because each format can produce multiple pages of output, this counter simply counts them.

Example

```
select(EG_FORMAT);
$one = $%;
$two = $%;
$three = $%;
write;
select(STDOUT);
```

$FORMAT_TOP_NAME

Compliance

4 5 NT

Syntax

Short Name `$^`
Scope `always global`
File Handle Call `format_top_name FILEHANDLE EXPR`

Definition

Each format can have an associated format that is reproduced each time a new page is generated. (No equivalent automatic page footer exists.) By default, these are given the same name as the base format with a `TOP` suffix, although any name can be set.

Example

```
format EG_TOP =
           [Sample Page Header]
To the left  In the center To the right
------------------
.
```

```
open(EG_FORMAT,">-");
select(EG_FORMAT);
$- = 0;
$^ = EG_TOP;
$one = '111';
$two = '222';
$three = '333';
$fitme= "";
write;
write;
write;
select(STDOUT);
```

$INPLACE_EDIT

Compliance

4 5 NT

Syntax

Short Name `$^I`
Scope `localize`

Definition

Perl is often used to edit files, and sometimes, the input file is also the output file (the result replaces the original). In this case, you can specify (with command-line options) the suffix to be used for the temporary file created while the edits are in progress. You can set or simply access this value from within the script itself by using this variable.

Example

```
$^I=bak;
print "Tmp file extension when editing in place...
     $^I\n";
```

$INPUT_LINE_NUMBER

Compliance

4 5 NT

Syntax

Short Name `$.`
Intermediate Name `$NR`
Scope `localize` *(read-only)*
File Handle Call `input_line_number FILEHANDLE EXPR`

Definition

This variable counts the number of lines of input from a file and is reset when the file is closed. The variable counts lines cumulatively across all input files read with the <> construct because these are not closed explicitly.

Example

```
print "The last file read had $. lines\n";
```

$INPUT_RECORD_SEPARATOR

Compliance

4 5 NT

Syntax

Short Name `$/`
Intermediate Name `$RS`
Scope `localize`
File Handle Call `input_record_separator FILEHANDLE EXPR`

Definition

By default, an input file is split into records, each of which comprises one line. The input-record separator is a newline character. This variable can be set to have no value (in which case entire input files are read in at the same time) or to have other values, as required.

Example

```
undef $/;
 open(INFILE,"infile.tst");
 $buffer = <INFILE>;
 print "$buffer\n";
```

$LAST_PAREN_MATCH

Compliance

4 5 NT

Syntax

Short Name `$+`
Scope `local`

Definition

This variable returns the value of the last pattern marked with parentheses. In most contexts, you could simply use `$1`, `$2`, and so on rather than `$+`. When the pattern has a series of sets of parentheses as alternatives to be matched, using `$+` is useful.

Example

```
$_ = "AlphaBetaDeltaGamma";
/Alpha(.*)Delta(.*)/;
print "The last match was $+\n";
```

$LIST_SEPARATOR

Compliance

4 5 NT

Syntax

Short Name `$"`
Scope `localize`

Definition

When arrays are converted to strings, the elements are separated by spaces by default, which, for example, is what happens when arrays are printed. This variable allows you to specify any string as the list separator, which may be useful for output formatting or for other reasons.

Example

```
$" = ' ! ';
@thisarray = (Alpha, Beta, Gamma);
print "@thisarray.\n";
$" = ' ';
```

$MATCH

Compliance

4 5 NT

Syntax

Short Name `$&`
Scope `local` *(read-only)*

Definition

This variable references the entire pattern that matched the most recent pattern matching operation.

Example

```
$_ = "AlphaBetaGamma";
/B[aet]*/;
print "Matched: $&\n";
```

$MULTILINE_MATCHING

Compliance

4 5 NT

Syntax

Short Name: `$*`
Scope: `localize`

Definition

By default, Perl optimizes pattern matching on the assumption that each pattern does not contain embedded newlines; that is, it is optimized for single-line matching. If you are using a pattern that has embedded newlines, you should set this variable to a value of 1 so that this optimization is disabled and the correct result is obtained.

Example

```
print("\nTest 26 Perl Version ($])\n");
$_ = "Alpha\nBeta\nGamma\n";
$* = 0; # Assume string comprises a single line
/^.*$/;
print "a) Assuming single line: $& ";
print "(which is wrong - the assumption was
wrong).\n";
```

```
$* = 1; # Do not assume string comprises a single
line
/^.*$/;
print "a) Not assuming single line: $& (which is
correct).\n";
$* = 0;
```

$OFMT

Compliance

4 5 NT

Syntax

Short Name `$#`
Scope `localize`

Definition

This variable mimics the UNIX `awk` utility variable of the same name, which permits numeric formatting. The default value is

```
%.2g
```

See the UNIX `awk` documentation for information about the possible values.

Example

```
$# = "%.6g";
print 5467.4567, "\n";
$# = "%.8g";
print 5467.4567, "\n";
```

TIP Use of the `$OFMT` variable is discouraged. You can format values by using the `print()` function.

$OS_ERROR

Compliance

4 5 NT

Syntax

Short Name `$!`
Intermediate Name `$ERRNO`
Scope `localize`

Definition

If an operating-system-error condition exists, this variable is set to the error number and, if it is evaluated in a string context, to the equivalent error message. You can manually set the error number and then access the relevant error message in a string context.

Example

```
ls -lgd /vir\;
print "OS Error was $!\n";
```

$OUTPUT_AUTOFLUSH

Compliance

4 5 NT

Syntax

Short Name `$|`
Scope `always global`
File Handle Call `autoflush FILEHANDLE EXPR`

Definition

If this Boolean variable, which is associated with a file handle, has a nonzero value, that file is autoflushed (the output is written after each print or write operation) rather than being buffered.

TIP When the output file is a pipe, it is best to set autoflush on so that other programs can access the pipe immediately after each write or print operation.

Example

```
select(STDERR);
$| = 1;
select(STDOUT);
print "Autoflush setting for STDOUT is $|\n";
```

$OUTPUT_FIELD_SEPARATOR

Compliance

4 5 NT

Syntax

Short Name `$,`
Intermediate Name `$OFS`
Scope `localize`
File Handle Call `output_field_separator FILEHANDLE EXPR`

Definition

This variable can alter the behavior of the `print()` function. The default behavior of `print()`, when it is given a comma-separated list of arguments, is to print each argument with no output separator. You can use this variable to specify any string as a separator.

Example

```
$, = "=";
print STDOUT a, b, c, "\n";
$, = "";
```

$OUTPUT_RECORD_SEPARATOR

Compliance

4 5 NT

Syntax

Short Name `$\`
Intermediate Name `$ORS`
Scope `localize`
File Handle Call `output_record_separator FILEHANDLE EXPR`

Definition

This variable can alter the behavior of the `print()` function. The default behavior of `print()`, when it is given a comma-separated list of arguments, is to print each argument. If a newline is required at the end, you must add it explicitly. You can use this record-separator variable to specify any string as the end-of-record string, and you most commonly set it to the newline character to avert the need for explicit newlines.

Example

```
$\ = "\n";
print "No need for an explicit new line now.";
$\ = "";
```

$PERLDB

Compliance

4 5 NT

Syntax

Short Name `$^P`
Scope `localize`

Definition

This flag represents the debug level of the Perl script. Normally, `$PERLDB` is used internally by the debugger to disable debugging of the debugger script itself.

Example

```
print "Value of internal Boolean debug flag:
$^P\n";
```

$PERL_VERSION

Compliance

4 5 NT

Syntax

Short Name `$]`
Scope `localize`

Definition

This variable represents the version string that identifies the Perl version that is being run. You can assign a value to the variable, if necessary. In a numeric context, the variable evaluates to a number made up of the version plus the `(patch level/1000)`.

Example

```
$ver = $]+0;
print "So every test has tested the version $]
(numeric $ver).\n";
```

$POSTMATCH

Compliance

4 5 NT

Syntax

Short Name `$'`
Scope `local` *(read-only)*

Definition

When a string is matched by pattern, the pattern is actually split into three parts: the part of the string before the match, the part of the string that matched, and the part of the string after the match. Any of these parts could be empty, of course. This variable refers to the part of the string after the match.

Example

```
$_ = "AlphaBetaGamma";
/Beta/;
print "Postmatch = $'\n";
```

$PREMATCH

Compliance

4 5 NT

Syntax

Short Name `$``

Scope `local` *(read-only)*

Definition

When a string is matched by pattern, the pattern is actually split into three parts: the part of the string before the match, the part of the string that matched, and the part of the string after the match. Any of these parts could be empty, of course. This variable refers to the part of the string before the match.

Example

```
$_ = "AlphaBetaGamma";
/Beta/;
print "Prematch = $`\n";
```

$PROCESS_ID

Compliance

4 5 NT

Syntax

Short Name `$$`

Intermediate Name `$PID`

Scope `localize`

Definition

In systems that support multiple processes, Perl can identify the process number of the Perl script current process (that is the process which is executing the Perl script itself) via this variable.

Example

```
print "The process ID (PID) is: $$\n";
```

$PROGRAM_NAME

Compliance

4 5 NT

Syntax

Short Name `$0`
Scope `localize`

Definition

This variable contains the name of the Perl script that is being executed. You can alter this variable if you want the script to identify itself to the operating system as having a particular name.

Example

```
print "The program name is: $0\n";
```

$REAL_GROUP_ID

Compliance

4 5 NT

Syntax

Short Name `$(`
Intermediate Name `$GID`
Scope `localize`

Definition

In systems that support users and groups, as well as setting new users and groups within a process, Perl can access both the original and the effective user and group information. The real group variable provides access to a list of numbers that represent the real group identifiers (GIDs). Effective GIDs may be set using flags in the script or explicit calls to functions. This will not alter the real GIDs.

Example

```
print("The Real Group ID is a list of GIDs: $(\n");
```

$REAL_USER_ID

Compliance

4 5 NT

Syntax

Short Name `$<`
Intermediate Name `$UID`
Scope `localize`

Definition

In systems that support users and groups, as well as setting new users and groups within a process, Perl can access both the original and the effective user and group information. The real user variable provides access to a list of numbers that represent the real user identifier (UID). An effective UID may be set by flags on the script or explicit calls to functions. This does not alter the real UID.

Example

```
print("The Real User ID is a list of UID: $<\n");
```

$SUBSCRIPT_SEPARATOR

Compliance

4 5 NT

Syntax

Short Name `$;`
Intermediate Name `$SUBSEP`
Scope `localize`

Definition

This variable is used in emulating multidimensional arrays. The value must be one that is not used by any element in the array. The default value is `\034`.

Perl 5 directly supports multidimensional arrays directly, so the use of `$SUBSCRIPT_SEPARATOR ($;)` is not necessary.

$SYSTEM_FD_MAX

Compliance

4 5 NT

Syntax

Short Name `$^F`
Scope `localize`

Definition

By default, Perl treats three files as system files 0, 1, and 2—normally, `STDIN`, `STDOUT`, and `STDERR`. The value of `$^F` is 2 by default. System files are treated specially; in particular, the file descriptors are passed to `exec()` processes.

Thus, file descriptors that number greater than `$^F` are automatically closed to child processes.

Example

```
print "The default maximum file descriptors is
$^F\n";
```

$WARNING

Compliance

4 5 NT

Syntax

Short Name `$^W`
Scope `localize`

Definition

This variable is a Boolean warning flag that you normally set to `true` by using the command-line `-w` switch, although you can set it within the script, if necessary. When this variable is on, the Perl program reports more verbose warnings.

Example

```
print "Boolean warning flag is set to: $^W\n";
```

%ENV{<variable_name>, <variable_value>}

Compliance

4 5 NT

Syntax

Short Name `%ENV{<variable_name>,<variable_value>}`
Scope always global

Definition

This variable is an associative array that links the names of the environment variables to their values. This variable makes it easy to look up a value with the appropriate name.

Example

```
$tmp = $ENV{SHELL};
 print "The current SHELL is set to $tmp\n";
```

%INC{<file-name>,<file-load-status>}

Compliance

4 5 NT

Syntax

Short Name `%INC{<file-name>,<file-load-status>}`
Scope always global

Definition

This variable is an associate array that links the names of the required files to a status (whether they were successfully loaded). Normally, the Perl script itself uses this array to determine whether files have already been loaded so as to minimize the number of file loads that are carried out.

Example

```
require 'another.pl';
 $tmp = $INC{'another.pl'};
 print "The required file did exist: $tmp\n";
```

%SIG{<signal-name>,<signal-value>}

Compliance

4 5 NT

Syntax

Short Name `%SIG{<signal-name>,<signal-value>}`
Scope `always global`

Definition

This variable is an associative array that links the standard signals to values. These values dictate the way that the script processes those signals. You can assign signal-handling subroutines to certain signals or set the script to ignore certain signals.

Example

```
$SIG{'HUP'} = 'IGNORE';
print "This process now ignores hangup signals.\n";
```

@ARGV[<N>]

Compliance

4 5 NT

Syntax

Short Name `@ARGV[<N>]`
Scope `always global`

Definition

This variable is an array of the arguments passed to the script. Unlike the situation in the C language, the first element of this array is the first argument (not the program name). As the arguments are processed, the value of this variable can alter. As with all arrays you can specify each element with `<N>` referring to the element number.

Example

```
$Example46String = "There were $#ARGV arguments,
first argument was @ARGV[0]\n";
print $Example46String;
```

@INC[<N>]

Compliance

4 5 NT

Syntax

Short Name `@INC[<N>]`
Scope `always global`

@INC[<N>]

Definition

This variable is an array of the directories to search for included files. These directories are normally specified either at the command line when launching the Perl program or in an environment variable. As with all arrays you can specify each element with `<N>` referring to the element number.

Example

```
print "The possible include script directories are:
@INC\n";
```

OPERATORS

Perl has a range of operators, many of which are similar to the operators used in C. Also, many Perl functions can be used either as a unary operator or as a function. The difference in the syntax is that the function call has parentheses enclosing the parameters. The difference in semantics is that the function form has a higher precedence. All such operators are listed as functions rather than as operators in this book.

This chapter categorizes each operator in several ways:

- Name   Unlike the special variables, no standard long form exists for the name of each operator. You must use the symbolic name.
- Precedence   Each operator is categorized with a precedence number, the lowest number being the highest precedence. Higher-precedence operations are evaluated before lower-precedence operations.
- Associativity   Each operator may be left, right, or nonassociative. This determines the order in which operands are evaluated.
- Type of Operands   This category indicates whether the operator operates on numeric or string arguments, lists, or files.
- Number of Operands   Each operator can operate on one (unary), two (binary), or three (ternary) operands. (Some operators operate on a list of operands—the list being of arbitrary length.)
- Context   Each operator can expect an array or a scalar context. Some operators have separate behaviors for each context.

The following lists the precedence of the operators:

1. `TERMs`, `LIST` operators (leftward)
2. `->`
3. ++ –
4. `**`

5. ! ~ - (unary) + (unary)
6. =~ !~
7. * / % x
8. + (binary) - (binary) .
9. << >>
10. NAMED unary operators
11. < > <= >= lt gt le ge
12. == != <=> eq ne cmp
13. &
14. | ^
15. &&
16. ||
17. ..
18. ?:
19. = += -= *= /= %= |= &= ^= <<= >>= **= ||= &&= .= |= x=
20. , =>
21. LIST operators (rightward)
22. not
23. and
24. or xor

This chapter contains detailed descriptions of these operators.

You may easily confuse some variables with some operators, so check the "Special Variables" chapter if the symbol is not described here.

Be aware that all Perl 5 (and many Perl 4) functions can behave as operators and as functions. The difference is in the syntax; functions have parentheses—as in `example()`. Operators which have a name rather than a symbol have been treated as functions and are covered in the "Functions" chapter (this includes the file-test operators `-f` and so on and the pattern matching operators `m//` and so on.).

!

Compliance

4 5 NT

Name Logical negation
Precedence 5
Associativity Right
Type of Operands Numeric, string
Number of Operands One (unary)
Context Scalar

Definition

The return value of this operation is 1 (true) if the operand has a false value that is defined as 0 in a numeric operand, a null string, or an undefined value. Otherwise, the return value is '' (false), that is, a null string that evaluates to 0 in a numeric context.

Example

```
$one = !1;
$two = !22;
$three = !0;
$four = !'hello';
$five = !'';
print "1=$one, 2=$two, 3=$three, 4=$four, 5=$five,
  \n";
```

!=

Compliance

4 5 NT

Name Relational not equal to
Precedence 12

Associativity Nonassociative
Type of Operands String
Number of Operands Two (binary)
Context Scalar

Definition

The return value of this operation is 1 (true) if the string operands are not equal. The return value is ' ' (false) if the string operands are equal. Every character in the strings is compared based on the character codes.

Example

```
$tmp = "aaa ";
$ans = "aaa" != $tmp;
if ($ans)
     { print "true\n"; }
else
     { print "false\n"; }
```

!~

Compliance

4 5 NT

Name Bind pattern (with negation of return value)
Precedence 6
Associativity Left
Type of Operands String
Number of Operands Two (binary)
Context Scalar
See also: =~

Definition

This operator binds a pattern-matching operation to a string variable other than $. If the pattern match is successful, the return value is ' ' (false); if the pattern match is not successful, the return value is 1 (true).

Example

```
$tmp = "superduper";
if ($tmp !~ s/duper/dooper/)
     {print "Did not do a substitute, tmp still is:
$tmp\n";}
else
     {print "Did a substitute, tmp now is:
$tmp\n";}
```

%

Compliance

4 5 NT

Name Modulus
Precedence 7
Associativity Left
Type of Operands Numeric
Number of Operands Two (binary)
Context Scalar

Definition

The operands are converted to integers, if necessary. The left side is divided by the right side, and the integer remainder is returned.

Example

```
$ans = 48 % 5;
print "48 mod 4 is: $ans\n";
```

%=

Compliance

4 5 NT

Name Modulus assignment
Precedence 18
Associativity Right
Type of Operands Numeric
Number of Operands Two (binary)
Context Scalar

Definition

This operation, like all the extra assignment operations, is a way to make the evaluation of the arguments more efficient.

Example

```
$ans = 48;
$ans %= 5;
print "48 mod 4 is: $ans\n";
```

&

Compliance

4 5 NT

Name Bitwise and
Precedence 13
Associativity Left
Type of Operands Numeric (integer)
Number of Operands Two (binary)
Context Scalar

Definition

This operator performs a *bitwise and* on the binary representation of the two numeric operands; that is, each bit of the two operands are compared with a logical and operation and the resulting bits form the result.

Example

```
$ans = 456 & 111;
print "Bitwise and 456 & 111 is: $ans\n";
```

&&

Compliance

4 **5** **NT**

Name Symbolic logical and
Precedence 15
Associativity Left
Type of Operands Numeric, string
Number of Operands Two (binary)
Context Scalar

Definition

As in all logical operations, a null string and zero are false. This operator returns `1` (true) if both of the operands are true or `null` (false) if either operand is false or both operands are false.

Example

```
$ans = 1 && print("This will print.\n") && 0 &&
print("This won't print!\n");
if ($ans)
     {print("So it's all true!\n");}
else
     {print("So it's not all true. (expected)\n");}
```

&&=

Compliance

4 5 NT

Name Assignment logical and
Precedence 19
Associativity Right
Type of Operands Numeric, string
Number of Operands Two (binary)
Context Scalar

Definition

This operator is a combination of the logical and assignment operators. This operator is more efficient when a new value is being reassigned to the same variable because the reference needs to be computed only one time.

Example

```
$ans = 1;
$ans &&= "eggs" eq "eggs";
if ($ans)
     {print("It's as true as eggs is eggs.
(expected)\n");}
else
     {print("Not true, I'm afraid.");}
```

&=

Compliance

4 5 NT

Name Assignment bitwise and
Precedence 19

Associativity Right
Type of Operands Numeric (integer)
Number of Operands Two (binary)
Context Scalar

Definition

This operator is a combination of the bitwise and assignment operators. This operator is more efficient when a new value is being reassigned to the same variable because the reference needs to be computed only one time.

Example

```
$ans = 456;
$ans &= 111;
print("Bitwise and 456 & 111 is $ans\n");
```

*

Compliance

4 5 NT

Name Multiplication
Precedence 7
Associativity Left
Type of Operands Numeric
Number of Operands Two (binary)
Context Scalar

Definition

This operator returns the numeric result of multiplying the two numeric operands.

Example

```
$ans = 7 * 10;
print("$ans (expected 70)\n");
```

**

Compliance

4 5 NT

Name Exponentiation
Precedence 4
Associativity Right
Type of Operands Numeric
Number of Operands Two (binary)
Context Scalar

Definition

The operation $x**y$ returns the value of x raised to the power of y.

Example

```
$ans = 2 ** 3;
print ("$ans (expected 8)\n");
```

**=

Compliance

4 5 NT

Name Assignment exponentiation
Precedence 19
Associativity Right
Type of Operands Numeric
Number of Operands Two (binary)
Context Scalar

Definition

This operator is a combination of the exponentiation and assignment operators. This operator is more efficient when a new value is being reassigned to the same variable because the reference needs to be computed only one time.

Example

```
$ans = 2;
$ans **= 3;
print ("$ans (expected 8)\n");
```

*=

Compliance

4 **5** **NT**

Name Assignment multiplication
Precedence 19
Associativity Right
Type of Operands Numeric
Number of Operands Two (binary)
Context Scalar

Definition

This operator is a combination of the multiplication and assignment operators. This operator is more efficient when a new value is being reassigned to the same variable because the reference needs to be computed only one time.

Example

```
$ans = 7;
$ans *= 10;
print ("$ans (expected 70)\n");
```

+ (Unary)

Compliance

4 5 NT

Name Unary plus
Precedence 5
Associativity Right
Type of Operands Numeric, string
Number of Operands One (unary)
Context Scalar

Definition

This operator does not actually have any operation on a numeric or a string operand. In certain circumstances, the operator can disambiguate an expression. When a parenthesis follows a function name, it is taken to indicate a complete list of the arguments to the function, unless the parenthesis is preceded by + to make the parenthesized expression just one of the list arguments for that function.

Example

```
@ans = sort +(5 + 5) * 10, -4;
print("@ans (expected 100, -4)\n");
```

+ (Binary)

Compliance

4 5 NT

Name Addition
Precedence 8
Associativity Left
Type of Operands Numeric

Number of Operands `Two (binary)`
Context `Scalar`

Definition

This operator returns the sum of the two operands.

Example

```
$ans = 15 + 5;
print("$ans (expected 20)\n");
```

++

Compliance

4 5 NT

Name `Autoincrement`
Precedence `3`
Associativity `Nonassociative`
Type of Operands `Numeric, string`
Number of Operands `One (unary)`
Context `Scalar`

Definition

In a numeric context, the autoincrement adds 1 to the operand. If the `syntax` is used as a prefix, the value before the increment is returned. If the `syntax` is used as a postfix, the value after the increment is returned.

With a string operand (that has never been used in a numeric context), the autoincrement has a "magic" behavior. If the string is an alphanumeric expression, such as `/^[a-zA-Z]*[0-9]*$/`, the increment is carried out on the string, including a carry (that is, the string "19" becomes "20" automatically just as if it were an integer).

Example

```
$ans = 45;
print $ans,   " (expected 45) ";
```

```
print $ans++, " (expected 45) ";
print ++$ans, " (expected 47)\n";
```

+=

Compliance

4 5 NT

Name Assignment addition
Precedence 19
Associativity Right
Type of Operands Numeric
Number of Operands Two (binary)
Context Scalar

Definition

This operator is a combination of the summation and assignment operators. This operator is more efficient when a new value is being reassigned to the same variable because the reference needs to be computed only one time.

Example

```
$ans = 15;
$ans += 5;
print("$ans (expected 20)\n");
```

,

Compliance

4 5 NT

Name Comma
Precedence 20

Associativity Left
Type of Operands Numeric, string
Number of Operands Two (binary)
Context Scalar, list

Definition

In a scalar context, the comma operator evaluates the operand to the left, discards the result, evaluates the operand to the right, and returns that value as the result.

In an array context, the comma operator separates items in the list. The operator behaves as though it returns both operands as part of the list.

Example

```
$ans = ('one', 'two', 'three');
print("$ans (expected three)\n");
```

- (Unary)

Compliance

4 5 NT

Name Negation
Precedence 5
Associativity Right
Type of Operands Numeric, string, identifier
Number of Operands One (unary)
Context Scalar

Definition

This operator returns the negated value of a numeric operand. If the operand is a string that begins with a plus or minus sign, the operator returns a string that has the opposite sign. If the argument is an identifier, the operator returns a string that comprises the identifier prefixed with a minus sign.

Example

```
$ans = 45;
$ans = -$ans;
print("$ans (expected -45)\n");
```

- (Binary)

Compliance

4 5 NT

Name Subtraction
Precedence 8
Associativity Left
Type of Operands Numeric
Number of Operands Two (binary)
Context Scalar

Definition

This operator returns the first operand minus the second operand.

Example

```
$ans = 50 - 10;
print("$ans (expected 40)\n");
```

--

Compliance

4 5 NT

Name Autodecrement
Precedence 3
Associativity Nonassociative

Type of Operands Numeric
Number of Operands One (unary)
Context Scalar

Definition

This operator decrements its operand. It also returns a value, but you have the choice to return the existing value (before any decrement takes place) or to return the new value (after the decrement takes place) by using the prefix notation or the postfix notation. So if $x is 56, —$x returns 56 and $x— returns 55, though in both cases the new value of $x is 55. This subtle difference is often important when one wants to both decrement a value and perform a test (for example with conditions in a loop).

Unlike the autoincrement operator, ++, this operator does not operate on strings.

Example

```
$ans = 45;
print $ans,   " (expected 45) ";
print $ans--, " (expected 45) ";
print --$ans, " (expected 43)\n";
```

-=

Compliance

4 **5** **NT**

Name Assignment subtraction
Precedence 19
Associativity Right
Type of Operands Numeric
Number of Operands Two (binary)
Context Scalar

Definition

This operator is a combination of the subtraction and assignment operators. This operator is more efficient when a new value is being reassigned to the same variable because the reference needs to be computed only one time.

Example

```
$ans = 50;
$ans -= 10;
print("$ans (expected 40)\n");
```

->

Compliance

5 NT

Name Dereference
Precedence 2
Associativity Left
Type of Operands Special
Number of Operands Two (binary)
Context Scalar, array

Definition

This operator is new to Perl 5. The capability to create and manipulate complex data types with references provides flexibility in Perl 5 that was not present in Perl 4. This operator is just one of the aspects of this functionality.

The operands for this operator can be

- A right side comprising array brackets or braces (`[]` or `{}`), and a left side comprising a reference to an array (or hash).
- A right side comprising a method name (or a variable with a method name), and a left side of either an object or a class name.

The operator allows you to access the elements in the data structure referenced by the left side (an array name, a hash name, an object, or a class name). Because there is no automatic dereferencing, you must use this syntax to dereference such a reference.

Example

```
@ans = (100, 200, 300);
$ansref = \@ans;
$ansref->[2] = 400;
print $ans[2], " (expected 400)\n";
```

◆

Compliance

4 5 NT

Name String concatenation
Precedence 8
Associativity Left
Type of Operands String
Number of Operands Two (binary)
Context Scalar

Definition

This operator joins the two string operands, returning a longer string.

Example

```
$ans = "jordy" . " jordy";
print $ans, " (expected jordy jordy)\n";
```

Compliance

4 5 NT

Name Range operator
Precedence 17
Associativity Nonassociative
Type of Operands Numeric, string
Number of Operands Two (binary)
Context Scalar, list

Definition

In a list context, the range operator returns an array of values, starting from the left operand up to the right operand in steps of one. In this context, the range operator can use "magic" increments to increment strings, as with the autoincrement operator (++).

In a scalar context, the range operator returns a Boolean value. In effect, the return value remains false as long as the left operand is false. When the left operand becomes true, it becomes true until the right operand is true, after which it becomes false again.

The range operator can be used in a scalar context to set conditions for certain ranges of line numbers of an input file. This works because the default behavior when either operand is numeric is to compare that operand with the current line number (the `$INPUT_LINE_NUMBER` or `$.` special variable). Thus, it is easy using this construct to treat certain lines in an input file differently (in the following example, the first five lines of the input file are supressed from being output).

Example

```
@ans = 1..5;
print("@ans (expected 12345)\n");
open(INFILE,"<infile.tst");
while(<INFILE>) {
     print unless (1..5);
}
```

.=

Compliance

4 5 NT

Name Assignment concatenation
Precedence 19
Associativity Right
Type of Operands String
Number of Operands Two (binary)
Context Scalar

Definition

This operator is a combination of the concatenation and assignment operators. This operator is more efficient when a new value is being reassigned to the same variable because the reference needs to be computed only one time.

Example

```
$ans = "jordy";
$ans .= " jordy";
print $ans, " (expected jordy jordy)\n";
```

/

Compliance

4 5 NT

Name Division
Precedence 7
Associativity Left
Type of Operands Numeric
Number of Operands Two (binary)
Context Scalar

Definition

This operator returns the product of the operands.

Example

```
$ans = 10/2;
print(“$ans (expected 5)\n”);
```

/=

Compliance

4 5 NT

Name Assignment division
Precedence 19
Associativity Right
Type of Operands Numeric
Number of Operands Two (binary)
Context Scalar

Definition

This operator is a combination of the division and assignment operators. This operator is more efficient when a new value is being reassigned to the same variable because the reference needs to be computed only one time.

Example

```
$ans = 10;
$ans /= 2;
print(“$ans (expected 5)\n”);
```

<

Compliance

4 5 NT

Name Numeric less then
Precedence 11
Associativity Nonassociative
Type of Operands Numeric
Number of Operands Two (binary)
Context Scalar

Definition

This operator returns `1` if the left operand is numerically less than the right operand; otherwise, it returns `null`.

Example

```
$ans = 45 < 36;
if ($ans)
     { print("True.\n");}
else
     { print("False. (expected)\n");}
```

<<

Compliance

4 5 NT

Name Bitwise shift left
Precedence 9
Associativity Left
Type of Operands Numeric (integer)
Number of Operands Two (binary)
Context Scalar

Definition

This operator shifts the operand left one bit in binary representation and returns the result. This is usually only used when processing some form of binary data. For example, it may be that a number is a representation of a series of flags (on/off Boolean values). One can use an integer of value 0 to 16 to represent five flags as the binary representation of all possible states ranges from 00000 to 11111 (this is 0 to F in hexedecimal). When processing data in this form, it is often useful to use the binary shift operators to access individual bits. If you find the number modulus 2, this is the value of the least significant bit (1 or 0). If you shift the number to the right by one, you effectively remove the least significant bit. If you shift by one to the left, you effectively add a new least significant bit with a value of zero (doubling the actual value of the variable). See also >> for an example using such flags.

Caution: Bit shift operators depend on the implemention of storage on the machine being used and so may not be portable.

Example

```
$ans = 1024<<1;
print("$ans (Bitwise left shift of 1024 by 1
place)\n");
```

<=

Compliance

4 5 NT

Name Numeric less than or equal to
Precedence 11
Associativity Nonassociative
Type of Operands Numeric
Number of Operands Two (binary)
Context Scalar

Definition

This operator returns 1 (true) if the left operand is numerically less than or equal to the right operand.

Example

```
$ans = 345 <= 345;
print("Comparing 345 <= 345 yields $ans. (expected
1 for true).\n");
```

<<=

Compliance

4 **5** **NT**

Name Assignment bitwise shift left
Precedence 19
Associativity Right
Type of Operands Numeric (integer)
Number of Operands Two (binary)
Context Scalar

Definition

This operator is a combination of the bitwise shift left and assignment operators. This operator is more efficient when a new value is being reassigned to the same variable because the reference needs to be computed only one time.

Example

```
$ans = 1024;
$ans <<= 1;
print("$ans (Bitwise left shift of 1024 by 1
place)\n");
```

<=>

Compliance

4 5 NT

Name Numeric comparison
Precedence 12
Associativity Nonassociative
Type of Operands Numeric
Number of Operands Two (binary)
Context Scalar

Definition

This operator returns `0` if the two numeric operands are equal. The operator returns `-1` if the left operand is less than the right operand and `+1` if the left operand is greater than the right operand.

Example

```
$ans = 345 <=> 347;
print("Comparing 345 with 437 yields $ans. (ex-
pected -1 for less than).\n");
```

=

Compliance

4 5 NT

Name Assignment
Precedence 19
Associativity Right
Type of Operands Numeric, string
Number of Operands Two (binary)
Context Scalar, list

Definition

In a scalar context, the assignment operator assigns the right operand's value to the variable specified by the left operand. The assignment operator returns the value of the variable.

In an array context, the assignment can assign multiple values to an array as the left operand if the right side results in a list.

Example

```
$ans = 43;
print("Assignment to \$ans: $ans (expected 43)\n");
```

==

Compliance

4 5 NT

Name Numeric equality
Precedence 12
Associativity Nonassociative
Type of Operands Numeric
Number of Operands Two (binary)
Context Scalar

Definition

This operator returns `1` (true) if the left and right numeric operands are numerically equal; otherwise, it returns `null` (false).

Example

```
$ans = 345 == 347;
print("Comparing 345 with 347 yields +$ans+. (ex-
pected null not equal).\n");
```

=>

Compliance

4 5 NT

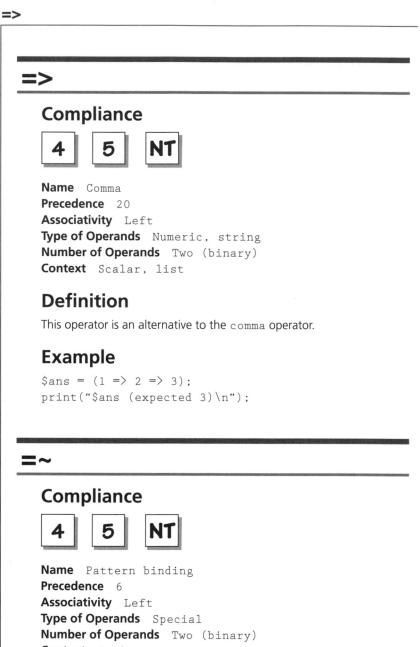

Name Comma
Precedence 20
Associativity Left
Type of Operands Numeric, string
Number of Operands Two (binary)
Context Scalar, list

Definition

This operator is an alternative to the `comma` operator.

Example

```
$ans = (1 => 2 => 3);
print("$ans (expected 3)\n");
```

=~

Compliance

4 5 NT

Name Pattern binding
Precedence 6
Associativity Left
Type of Operands Special
Number of Operands Two (binary)
Context Scalar

Definition

The default string matched by pattern-match operations is $_. Any other string can be bound to a pattern-matching operation using the pattern-binding operator. The left operand is a string to be searched. The right operand is a pattern-match operation (search, substitution, and translation). The return value is true or false, depending on the success of the operation.

Example

```
$tmp = "superduper";
if ($tmp =~ s/duper/dooper/)
     {print "Did do a substitute, tmp now is:
$tmp\n";}
else
     {print "Did not a substitute, tmp still is:
$tmp\n";}
```

>

Compliance

4 5 NT

Name `Numeric greater than`
Precedence `11`
Associativity `Nonassociative`
Type of Operands `Numeric`
Number of Operands `Two (binary)`
Context `Scalar`

Definition

This operator returns `1` (true) if the left numeric operand is greater than the right numeric operand; otherwise, it returns `null` (false).

Example

```
$ans = 45 > 36;
if ($ans)
     { print("True.\n");}
else
     { print("False. (expected)\n");}
```

>>

Compliance

4 5 NT

Name Bitwise shift right
Precedence 9
Associativity Left
Type of Operands Numeric (integer)
Number of Operands Two (binary)
Context Scalar

Definition

This operator shifts the operand right one bit in binary representation and returns the result. This is usually only used when processing some form of binary data. For example, it may be that a number is a representation of a series of flags (on/off Boolean values). One can use an integer of value 0 to 16 to represent five flags as the binary representation of all possible states ranges from 00000 to 11111 (this is 0 to F in hexedecimal). When processing data in this form, it is often useful to use the binary shift operators to access individual bits. If you find the number modulus 2, this is the value of the least significant bit (1 or 0). If you shift the number to the right by one, you effectively remove the least significant bit. If you shift by one to the left, you effectively add a new least significant bit with a value of zero (doubling the actual value of the variable).

CAUTION Bit shift operators depend on the implemention of storage on the machine being used and so may not be portable.

Example

```
$flags = 10; # i.e. Binary 01010 list of flags
for ($i=0;$i<=4;$i++) {
     # shift to make bit we want least significant
(rightmost)
     # then find this modulus 2 to test this bit
     # (NB bit shift operations may not be por-
table)
     ($flags>>$i)%2 ? print "$i on\n" : print "$i
off\n";
```

>=

Compliance

4 **5** **NT**

Name Numeric greater than or equal to
Precedence 11
Associativity Nonassociative
Type of Operands Numeric
Number of Operands Two (binary)
Context Scalar

Definition

This operator returns `1` (true) if the left numeric operand is greater than or equal to the right numeric operand; otherwise, it returns `null` (false).

Example

```
$ans = 345 >= 345;
print("Comparing 345 >= 345 yields $ans. (expected
1 for true).\n");
```

>>=

Compliance

4 5 NT

Name Assignment bitwise shift right
Precedence 19
Associativity Left
Type of Operands Numeric (integer)
Number of Operands Two (binary)
Context Scalar

Definition

This operator is a combination of the bitwise shift right and assignment operators. This operator is more efficient when a new value is being reassigned to the same variable because the reference needs to be computed only one time.

Example

```
$ans = 1024;
$ans >>= 1;
print("$ans (Bitwise right shift of 1024 by 1
place)\n");
```

?:

Compliance

4 5 NT

Name Conditional operator
Precedence 18
Associativity Right
Type of Operands Numeric, string
Number of Operands Three (ternary)

Context `Scalar, list`

Definition

This operator is like a symbolic `if...then...else` clause. If the left operand is true, the center operand is returned; otherwise, the right operand is returned. Either of the operands can return scalar or list values, and these values will be returned if the context allows.

Example

```
$ans = (45 == 45) ? “Equal (expected).\n” : “Not
equal.\n”;
print $ans;
```

LIST Operators (Leftward)

Compliance

4 5 NT

Name `All named list operators`
Precedence `1`
Associativity `Left`
Type of Operands `Special`
Number of Operands `List`
Context `List`

Definition

Several functions require a list as a parameter. The list may be written with or without the function parentheses. These list functions are in fact operators that behave like functions when their arguments are in parentheses. If they are written with parentheses, everything within the parentheses is taken as the list argument to the function, and they behave as a `TERM`.

When the function call is written without parentheses, the precedence is slightly more complex. The list operator has a different precedence, depending on whether the comparison is to the left of the list operator (leftward) or to the right of the list operator (rightward). The list operator has higher or equal precedence compared with all operators to its left. Thus, in the following example, `join` is evaluated before `print` because `print` is to the left of `join`.

Example

```
print 'Ones ', 'Twos ', join 'hoho ', 'Threes ',
'Fours ', "\n";
```

LIST Operators (Rightward)

Compliance

4 5 NT

Name `All named list operators`
Precedence `21`
Associativity `Nonassociative`
Type of Operands `Special`
Number of Operands `List`
Context `List`

Definition

Several functions require a list as a parameter. The list can be written with or without the function parentheses. These functions are in fact operators that behave like functions when their arguments are in parentheses. If they are written with parentheses, everything within the parentheses is taken as the list argument to the function, and they behave as a `TERM`.

When the function is written without parentheses, the precedence is slightly more complex. The list operator has a different precedence, depending on whether the comparison is to the left of the list operator (leftward) or to the right of the list operator (rightward). The list operator has lower or equal precedence compared with all operators to its right. Thus, in the following example, `print` is evaluated after `join` because `join` is to the right of `print`.

Example

```
print 'Ones ', 'Twos ', join 'hoho ', 'Threes ',
'Fours ', "\n";
```

NAMED Unary Operators

Compliance

4 5 NT

Name All named unary operators
Precedence 10
Associativity Nonassociative
Type of Operands Special
Number of Operands One (unary)
Context Scalar

Definition

In a similar way to list operators, NAMED unary operators can behave as a TERM by being expressed with a function syntax, with the argument placed in parentheses.

When the function is written without parentheses, the precedence of these operators is lower than arithmetic types of operators but greater than the symbolic string and numeric comparisons. Thus, in the following example, the first int takes the result of the arithmetic division 7/2 as its argument, so 3 is printed. The second int is a term bound to 7, which returns 7 and then is divided by 2 to yield 3.5.

Example

```
print 'Ones ', 'Twos ', int 7/2, (int 7)/2,
' Fours', "\n";
```

TERMs

Compliance

4 5 NT

Name TERMs
Precedence 1
Associativity Left
Type of Operands Special
Number of Operands N/A
Context N/A

Definition

A TERM can be any variable, any expression enclosed in parentheses, any function with its arguments in parentheses, and also a quoted expression (using the so-called "quote" and "quotelike" operators). TERMs have the highest possible precedence; in other words, they are replaced by their return value when the entire expression is being evaluated before any other operator of lower precedence is evaluated. TERMs appear in this chapter to show where they fall in the order of precedence.

Example

```
print 'One ', (1, 2, 3), "(expect One 3)\n";
```

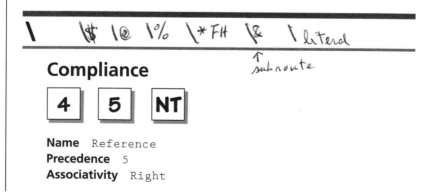

\

\$ \@ \% *FH \& \literal

↑ subroute

Compliance

4 5 NT

Name Reference
Precedence 5
Associativity Right

Type of Operands One (unary)
Number of Operands Special
Context Scalar

Definition

This operator permits the creation of references and the use of complex data types. One example is the capability to create another reference to an existing array variable.

```
@ans = (100, 200, 300);
$ansref = \@ans;
$ansref->[2] = 400;
print $ans[2], " (expected 400)\n";
```

^

Compliance

5 NT

Name Bitwise exclusive or
Precedence 14
Associativity Left
Type of Operands Two (binary)
Number of Operands Numeric (integer)
Context Scalar

Definition

This operator returns the result of a bitwise exclusive or on the two operands.

Example

```
$ans = 456 ^ 111;
print "Bitwise xor 456 & 111 is: $ans\n";
```

^=

Compliance

4 5 NT

Name Assignment bitwise exclusive or
Precedence 19
Associativity Right
Type of Operands Numeric (integer)
Number of Operands Two (binary)
Context Scalar

Definition

This operator is a combination of the bitwise exclusive or and assignment operators. This operator is more efficient when a new value is being reassigned to the same variable because the reference needs to be computed only one time.

Example

```
$ans = 456;
$ans ^= 111;
print "Bitwise xor 456 & 111 is: $ans\n";
```

and

Compliance

5 NT

Name And
Precedence 23
Associativity Left
Type of Operands Numeric, string

Number of Operands Two (binary)
Context Scalar

Definition

This operator is the lower-precedence version of &&.

Example

```
$ans = (1 and 3 || 0);
if ($ans)
     { print "true (expected)\n"; }
else
     { print "false\n"; }
```

cmp

Compliance

4 5 NT

Name String comparison
Precedence 12
Associativity Nonassociative
Type of Operands String
Number of Operands Two (binary)
Context Scalar

Definition

This operator compares two string operands and returns -1 if the first is less than the second, 0 if the operands are equal, and 1 if the first operand is greater than the second.

Example

```
$ans = "abc" cmp "aba";
print("Comparing (cmp) abc with aba yields $ans
(expected +1 aba > abc).\n");
```

eq

Compliance

4 5 NT

Name String equality
Precedence 12
Associativity Nonassociative
Type of Operands String
Number of Operands Two (binary)
Context Scalar

Definition

This operator tests whether two strings are equal, returning `1` (true) if they are and `null` (false) if they are not.

Example

```
$ans = "abc" eq "abc";
print("Comparing (eq) abc with abc yields $ans
(expected 1 true).\n");
```

ge

Compliance

4 5 NT

Name String greater than or equal to
Precedence 11
Associativity Nonassociative
Type of Operands String
Number of Operands Two (binary)
Context Scalar

Definition

This operator compares two strings and returns 1 (true) if the first string is greater than or equal to the second; otherwise, it returns null (false).

Example

```
$ans = "abc" ge "abc";
print("Comparing (ge) abc with abc yields $ans
(expected 1 true).\n");
```

gt

Compliance

4 5 NT

Name String greater than
Precedence 11
Associativity Nonassociative
Type of Operands String
Number of Operands Two (binary)
Context Scalar

Definition

This operator compares two strings and returns 1 (true) if the first is greater than the second; otherwise, it returns null (false).

Example

```
$ans = "abc" gt "aba";
print("Comparing (gt) abc with aba yields $ans
(expected 1 true).\n");
```

le

Compliance

4 5 NT

Name String less than or equal to
Precedence 11
Associativity Nonassociative
Type of Operands String
Number of Operands Two (binary)
Context Scalar

Definition

This operator compares two strings and returns `1` (true) if the first is less than or equal to the second; otherwise, it returns `null` (false).

Example

```
$ans = "abc" le "aba";
print("Comparing (le) abc with aba yields +$ans+
(expected null false).\n");
```

lt

Compliance

4 5 NT

Name String less than
Precedence 11
Associativity Nonassociative
Type of Operands String
Number of Operands Two (binary)
Context Scalar

Definition

This operator compares two strings and returns 1 (true) if the first is less than the second; otherwise, it returns null (false).

Example

```
$ans = "abc" lt "aba";
print("Comparing (lt) abc with aba yields +$ans+
(expected null false).\n");
```

ne

Compliance

4 5 NT

Name String not equal to
Precedence 12
Associativity Nonassociative
Type of Operands String
Number of Operands Two (binary)
Context Scalar

Definition

This operator compares two strings and returns 1 (true) if they are not equal; otherwise, it returns null (false).

Example

```
$ans = "abc" ne "aba";
print("Comparing (ne) abc with aba yields $ans
(expected 1 true).\n");
```

not

Compliance

5 NT

Name Not
Precedence 22
Associativity Right
Type of Operands Numeric, string
Number of Operands One (unary)
Context Scalar

Definition

This operator is the lower-precedence version of `!`.

Example

```
$ans = not 1;
print("Not 1 is +$ans+ (expected null)\n");
```

or

Compliance

5 NT

Name Or
Precedence 24
Associativity Left
Type of Operands Numeric, string
Number of Operands Two (binary)
Context Scalar

Definition

This operator is the lower-precedence version of `||`.

Example

```
open TSTFILE, "<nofile.txt" or print "The file
doesn't exist\n";
```

x

Compliance

4 5 NT

Name Repetition
Precedence 6
Associativity Left
Type of Operands String and numeric (integer)
Number of Operands Two (binary)
Context Scalar

Definition

The first operand must be a string, and the second operand must be an integer. The operator returns a string comprising the string operand repeated the specified number of times.

Example

```
print "Hello " x 5, "\n";
```

x=

Compliance

4 5 NT

Name Assignment repetition
Precedence 19

Associativity Right
Type of Operands String and numeric (integer)
Number of Operands Two (binary)
Context Scalar

Definition

This operator is a combination of the repetition and assignment operators. This operator is more efficient when a new value is being reassigned to the same variable because the reference needs to be computed only one time.

Example

```
$ans = 'Hello ';
$ans x= 5;
print("$ans\n");
```

xor

Compliance

5 **NT**

Name Exclusive or
Precedence 24
Associativity Left
Type of Operands Numeric, string
Number of Operands Two (binary)
Context Scalar

Definition

This operator returns `1` (true) or `null` (false) as an exclusive or of the two operands: the result is true if either but not both of the operands is true.

Example

```
for (0..1) {
      $a = $_;
      for (0..1) {
            $b = $_;
            print $a, ,' ', $b, ' ', ($a xor $b) ? 1
: 0, "\n";
            }
      }
```

|

Compliance

4 5 NT

Name Bitwise or
Precedence 14
Associativity Left
Type of Operands Numeric (integer)
Number of Operands Two (binary)
Context Scalar

Definition

This operator returns an integer that is the result of a bitwise or between the two integer operands.

Example

```
$ans = 2 | 1024;
print("2 OR 1204 is $ans\n");
```

||

Compliance

4 5 NT

Name Symbolic or
Precedence 11
Associativity Left
Type of Operands Numeric, string
Number of Operands Two (binary)
Context Scalar

Definition

This operator returns 1 (true) if either of the two operands is true and null (false) otherwise.

Example

```
$ans = '' || 'okay';
print("null || okay is $ans (expected okay
true)\n");
```

|=

Compliance

4 5 NT

Name Assignment bitwise or
Precedence 19
Associativity Right
Type of Operands Numeric (integer)
Number of Operands Two (binary)
Context Scalar

Definition

This operator is a combination of the bitwise or and assignment operators. This operator is more efficient when a new value is being reassigned to the same variable because the reference needs to be computed only one time.

Example

```
$ans = 2;
$ans |= 1024;
print("2 OR 1204 is $ans\n");
```

||=

Compliance

4 **5** **NT**

Name Assignment symbolic or
Precedence 19
Associativity Right
Type of Operands Numeric, string
Number of Operands Two (binary)
Context Scalar

Definition

This operator is a combination of the symbolic or and assignment operators. This operator is more efficient when a new value is being reassigned to the same variable because the reference needs to be computed only one time.

Example

```
$ans = '';
$ans ||= 'okay';
print("null || okay is $ans (expected okay
true)\n");
```

~

Compliance

4 5 NT

Name Bitwise not
Precedence 5
Associativity Right
Type of Operands Numeric (integer)
Number of Operands One (unary)
Context Scalar

Definition

This operator returns the bitwise negation of an integer operand. The result of this operation is sometimes known as the *one's complement*.

Example

```
$ans = ~1000000000;
print("Bitwise negation of 1000000000 is $ans\n");
```

FUNCTIONS

Perl has a large number of functions that come as standard with most implementations, and an even wider range of additional modules, each with its own additional functions. This chapter lists all the standard functions alphabetically for reference.

Each function is assigned a category. There are two main categories; list operators, which can take more than one argument, and named unary operators, which can only take one argument. A secondary category is noted in parentheses so you can see, at a glance, the type of operation the function performs. This is a very rough categorization, as many functions might overlap in any category scheme.

For each function the form of the arguments is listed. If there are multiple forms of calling the function, there will be multiple lines describing each form. The meanings of the arguments are described in the text.

The type of value returned by the function is listed. This is usually specified in more detail in the function description.

Two categories of functions, those dealing with sockets and those dealing with System V interprocess communications, are not dealt with in great detail. Both of these categories of function are direct counterparts of UNIX system functions.

The chapter includes

- A detailed description of each Perl function, ordered alphabetically.
- An example of the function's usage, where applicable.

-A

Compliance

4 5 NT

Syntax

Category named unary operator (file test)
Arguments handle
Arguments filename
Arguments none
Return Value integer (age of file in days since last access relative to $BASETIME)

Definition

The `file test` operator takes one file `handle` or `filename` as an argument. It returns `age of file in days since last access relative to $BASETIME`. All `file test` operators can take a special argument underscore, which means that the test is carried out on the same file `handle` as the last `file test`, `stat()`, or `lstat()` call. If no argument is supplied, `$_` is used.

Example

```
print "-A ", -A "/etc/fstab", "\n";
```

-B

Compliance

4 5 NT

Syntax

Category named unary operator (file test)
Arguments handle
Arguments filename
Arguments none
Return Value 1 (true) '' (false)

Definition

The `file test` operator takes one file `handle` or `filename` as an argument. It returns `1` (true) if the file is binary. It returns `''` (false) if the file is not binary. The first characters of the file are checked to see if the high bit is set and if a suitable number do have the high bit set the file is assumed to be binary. If the file is empty it is returned as binary. Because this test involves reading the file itself, it is best to test to learn if the file exists as a plain file (`-f`), first. All `file test` operators can take a special argument underscore, which means that the test is carried out on the same file `handle` as the last `file test`, `stat()`, or `lstat()` call. If no argument is supplied, `$_` is used.

Example

```
(-B "/etc/fstab") ? print("-B fstab is binary\n") :
    print("-B fstab is not binary\n");
```

-b

Compliance

4 5 NT

Syntax

Category `named unary operator (file test)`
Arguments `handle`
Arguments `filename`
Arguments `none`
Return Value `1 (true) '' (false)`

Definition

The `file test` operator takes one file `handle` or `filename` as an argument. It returns `1` (true) if the file is a block special file (that is, a UNIX `/dev` device file). It returns `''` (false) if the file is not a block special file. All `file test` operators can take a special argument underscore, which means that the test is carried out on the same file `handle` as the last `file test`, `stat()`, or `lstat()` call. If no argument is supplied, `$_` is used.

Example

```
(-b "/dev/hda1") ? print("-b hda1 is block\n") :
   print("-b hda1 is not block\n");
```

-C

Compliance

4 5 NT

Syntax

Category named unary operator (file test)
Arguments handle
Arguments filename
Arguments none
Return Value integer (age of file in days since last inode change relative to $BASETIME)

Definition

The `file test` operator takes one file `handle` or `filename` as an argument. It returns `age of file in days since last inode change relative to $BASETIME`. All `file test` operators can take a special argument underscore, which means that the test is carried out on the same file `handle` as the last `file test`, `stat()`, or `lstat()` call. If no argument is supplied, `$_` is used.

Example

```
print "-C ", -C "/etc/fstab", "\n";
```

-c

Compliance

4 5 NT

Syntax

Category `named unary operator (file test)`
Arguments `handle`
Arguments `filename`
Arguments `none`
Return Value `1 (true) '' (false)`

Definition

The `file test` operator takes one file `handle` or `filename` as an argument. It returns `1` (true) if the file is a character special file. It returns `''` (false) if the file is not a character special file. All `file test` operators can take a special argument underscore, which means that the test is carried out on the same file `handle` as the last `file test`, `stat()`, or `lstat()` call. If no argument is supplied, `$_` is used.

Example

```
(-c "/dev/tty0") ? print("-c tty0 is char\n") :
   print("-c tty0 is not char\n");
```

-d

Compliance

4 5 NT

Syntax

Category named unary operator (file test)
Arguments handle
Arguments filename
Arguments none
Return Value 1 (true) '' (false)

Definition

The file test operator takes one file handle or filename as an argument. It returns 1 (true) if the file is a directory. It returns '' (false) if the file is not a directory. All file test operators can take a special argument underscore, which means that the test is carried out on the same file handle as the last file test, stat(), or lstat() call. If no argument is supplied, $_ is used.

Example

```
(-d "/") ? print("-d / is dir\n") : print("-d / is
not dir\n");
```

-e

Compliance

4 5 NT

Syntax

Category named unary operator (file test)
Arguments handle
Arguments filename
Arguments none
Return Value 1 (true) '' (false)

Definition

The `file test` operator takes one file `handle` or `filename` as an argument. It returns `1` (true) if file exists. It returns `''` (false) if the file does not exist. All `file test` operators can take a special argument underscore, which means that the test is carried out on the same file `handle` as the last `file test`, `stat()`, or `lstat()` call. If no argument is supplied, `$_` is used.

Example

```
(-e "/") ? print("-e / exists\n") : print("-e /
exists\n");
```

-f

Compliance

4 **5** **NT**

Syntax

Category `named unary operator (file test)`
Arguments `handle`
Arguments `filename`
Arguments `none`
Return Value `1 (true) '' (false)`

Definition

The `file test` operator takes one file `handle` or `filename` as an argument. It returns `1` (true) if the file is a plain file. It returns `''` (false) if the file is not a plain file. A plain file is any file that is not a special block device (`-b`), a special character device (`-c`), a directory (`-d`), a symbolic link (`-l`), a pipe (`-p`), a named socket (`-S`), or a direct link to an I/O terminal (`-t`). All `file test` operators can take a special argument underscore, which means that the test is carried out on the same file `handle` as the last `file test`, `stat()`, or `lstat()` call. If no argument is supplied, `$_` is used.

Example

```
(-f "/") ? print("-f / is plain\n") : print("-f /
    is not plain\n");
```

-g

Compliance

4 5 NT

Syntax

Category named unary operator (file test)
Arguments handle
Arguments filename
Arguments none
Return Value 1 (true) '' (false)

Definition

The `file test` operator takes one file `handle` or `filename` as an argument. It returns `1` (true) if the file has the `setgid` bit set. It returns `''` (false) if the file does not have the `setgid` bit set. In UNIX, `setgid` allows an executable to run as if it was being run by the group, which owns the executable itself while executing (for example, if a binary is owned by the group `wwwstat`, and the binary has the `getgid` bit set, then that binary has access to all files that the `wwwstat` group can access while the binary is running, even when the binary is run by someone who is not actually a member of the `wwwstat` group). All `file test` operators can take a special argument underscore, which means that the test is carried out on the same file `handle` as the last `file test`, `stat()`, or `lstat()` call. If no argument is supplied, `$_` is used.

Example

```
(-g "/vmlinuz") ? print("-g /vmlinuz has setgid\n") :
    print("-g /vmlinuz has not setgid\n");
```

-k

Compliance

4 5 NT

Syntax

Category `named unary operator (file test)`
Arguments `handle`
Arguments `filename`
Arguments `none`
Return Value `1 (true) '' (false)`

Definition

The `file test` operator takes one file `handle` or `filename` as an argument. It returns `1` (true) if the sticky bit is set. It returns `''` (false) if the sticky bit is not set. In UNIX, the sticky bit can mark an executable file to be held in memory when exited (for example, if the binary `ls` is marked as sticky, when the first person runs it, it is loaded from disk to memory and executed, but when the execution finishes, the binary stays in memory so that when the next person runs `ls` it does not need to be loaded into memory again because it is already there). This is normally set for frequently used commands to optimize execution speed. All `file test` operators can take a special argument underscore, which means that the test is carried out on the same file `handle` as the last `file test`, `stat()`, or `lstat()` call. If no argument is supplied, `$_` is used.

Example

```
(-k "/vmlinuz") ? print("-k /vmlinuz is sticky\n") :
   print("-k /vmlinuz is not sticky\n");
```

-l

Compliance

4 5 NT

Syntax

Category `named unary operator (file test)`
Arguments `handle`
Arguments `filename`
Arguments `none`
Return Value `1 (true) '' (false)`

Definition

The `file test` operator takes one file `handle` or `filename` as an argument. It returns `1` (true) if the file is a symbolic link. It returns `''` (false) if the file is not a symbolic link. All `file test` operators can take a special argument underscore, which means that the test is carried out on the same file `handle` as the last `file test`, `stat()`, or `lstat()` call. If no argument is supplied, `$_` is used.

Example

```
(-l "/vmlinuz") ? print("-l /vmlinuz is symlink\n") :
    print("-l /vmlinuz is not symlink\n");
```

-M

Compliance

4 5 NT

Syntax

Category `named unary operator (file test)`
Arguments `handle`
Arguments `filename`
Arguments `none`
Return Value `integer (age of file in days relative to $BASETIME)`

Definition

The `file test` operator takes one file `handle` or `filename` as an argument. It returns the `age of the file in days relative to $BASETIME`. All `file test` operators can take a special argument underscore, which means that the test is carried out on the same file `handle` as the last `file test`, `stat()`, or `lstat()` call. If no argument is supplied, `$_` is used.

Example

```
print "-M ", -M "/etc/fstab", "\n";
```

-O

Compliance

4 **5** **NT**

Syntax

Category `named unary operator (file test)`
Arguments `handle`
Arguments `filename`
Arguments `none`
Return Value `1 (true) '' (false)`

Definition

The `file test` operator takes one file `handle` or `filename` as an argument. It returns `1` (true) if the file is owned by the real UID/GID and it returns '' (false) otherwise. For the superuser it always returns true. All `file test` operators can take a special argument underscore, which means that the test is carried out on the same file `handle` as the last `file test`, `stat()`, or `lstat()` call. If no argument is supplied, `$_` is used.

Example

```
(-o "/vmlinuz") ? print("-o /vmlinuz is owned by
   real uid/gid\n") :
   print("-o /vmlinuz is not owned by real uid/
      gid\n");
```

-O

Compliance

4 **5** **NT**

Syntax

Category named unary operator (file test)
Arguments handle
Arguments filename
Arguments none
Return Value 1 (true) '' (false)

Definition

The `file test` operator takes one file `handle` or `filename` as an argument. This function returns `1` (true) if the file is owned by the effective UID/GID and it returns '' (false) otherwise. For the superuser it always returns true. All `file test` operators can take a special argument underscore, which means that the test is carried out on the same file `handle` as the last `file test`, `stat()`, or `lstat()` call. If no argument is supplied, `$_` is used.

Example

```
(-O "/vmlinuz") ? print("-O /vmlinuz is owned by
   effective uid/gid\n") :
   print("-o /vmlinuz is not owned by effective
      uid/gid\n");
```

-p

Compliance

4 5 NT

Syntax

Category named unary operator (file test)
Arguments handle
Arguments filename
Arguments none
Return Value 1 (true) '' (false)

Definition

The `file test` operator takes one file `handle` or `filename` as an argument. It returns `1` (true) if the file is a named pipe. It returns `''` (false) if the file is not a named pipe. All `file test` operators can take a special argument underscore, which means that the test is carried out on the same file `handle` as the last `file test`, `stat()`, or `lstat()` call. If no argument is supplied, `$_` is used.

Example

```
(-p "/vmlinuz") ? print("-p /vmlinuz is named
   pipe\n") :
   print("-p /vmlinuz is not named pipe\n");
```

-R

Compliance

4 5 NT

Syntax

Category named unary operator (file test)
Arguments handle
Arguments filename
Arguments none
Return Value 1 (true) '' (false)

Definition

The `file test` operator takes one file `handle` or `filename` as an argument. It returns 1 (true) if the file is readable by the effective UID/GID and it returns '' (false) otherwise. For the superuser it always returns true. All `file test` operators can take a special argument underscore, which means that the test is carried out on the same file `handle` as the last `file test`, `stat()`, or `lstat()` call. If no argument is supplied, `$_` is used.

Example

```
(-R "/vmlinuz") ? print("-R /vmlinuz is readable by
     effective uid/gid\n") :
   print("-R /vmlinuz is not readable by effective
      uid/gid\n");
```

-r

Compliance

4 5 NT

Syntax

Category `named unary operator (file test)`
Arguments `handle`
Arguments `filename`
Arguments `none`
Return Value `1 (true) '' (false)`

Definition

The `file test` operator takes one file `handle` or `filename` as an argument. It returns `1` (true) if the file is readable by the real UID/GID and it returns `''` (false) otherwise. For the superuser it always returns true. All `file test` operators can take a special argument underscore, which means that the test is carried out on the same file `handle` as the last `file test`, `stat()`, or `lstat()` call. If no argument is supplied, `$_` is used.

Example

```
(-r "/vmlinuz") ? print("-r /vmlinuz is readable by
   real uid/gid\n") :
   print("-r /vmlinuz is not readable by real uid/
      gid\n");
```

-S

Compliance

4 5 NT

Syntax

Category `named unary operator (file test)`
Arguments `handle`
Arguments `filename`
Arguments `none`
Return Value `1 (true) '' (false)`

Definition

The file test operator takes one file handle or filename as an argument. It returns 1 (true) if the file is a symbolic link. It returns '' (false) if the file is not a symbolic link. All file test operators can take a special argument underscore, which means that the test is carried out on the same file handle as the last file test, stat(), or lstat() call. If no argument is supplied, $_ is used.

Example

```
(-S "/vmlinuz") ? print("-S /vmlinuz is socket\n") :
   print("-S /vmlinuz is not socket\n");
```

-s

Compliance

4 5 NT

Syntax

Category named unary operator (file test)
Arguments handle
Arguments filename
Arguments none
Return Value integer (size) '' (false)

Definition

The file test operator takes one file handle or filename as an argument. It returns size in bytes as an integer if the file has a non-zero size. It returns '' (false) if the file has zero size. All file test operators can take a special argument underscore, which means that the test is carried out on the same file handle as the last file test, stat(), or lstat() call. If no argument is supplied, $_ is used.

Example

```
(-s "/vmlinuz") ? print("-s /vmlinuz has non-zero
    size\n") :
   print("-s /vmlinuz does not have non-zero
       size\n");
```

-T

Compliance

4 5 NT

Syntax

Category `named unary operator (file test)`
Arguments `handle`
Arguments `filename`
Arguments `none`
Return Value `1 (true) '' (false)`

Definition

The `file test` operator takes one file `handle` or `filename` as an argument. It returns `1` (true) if the file is a text file. It returns `''` (false) if the file is not a text file. The first characters of the file are checked to see if the high bit is set, and if a suitable number are not set the file is assumed to be text. If the file is empty, true is returned. Because this test involves reading the file itself, it is best to test to learn if the file exists as a plain file (`-f`) first. All `file test` operators can take a special argument underscore, which means that the test is carried out on the same file `handle` as the last `file test`, `stat()`, or `lstat()` call. If no argument is supplied, `$_` is used.

Example

```
(-T "/vmlinuz") ? print("-T /vmlinuz is text
     file\n") :
   print("-T /vmlinuz is not text file\n");
```

-t

Compliance

4 | 5 | NT

Syntax

Category `named unary operator (file test)`
Arguments `handle`
Arguments `filename`
Arguments `none`
Return Value `1 (true) '' (false)`

Definition

The `file test` operator takes one file `handle` or `filename` as an argument. It returns `1` (true) if the file is a terminal `tty` device. It returns `''` (false) if the file is not. All `file test` operators can take a special argument underscore, which means that the test is carried out on the same file `handle` as the last `file test`, `stat()`, or `lstat()` call. If no argument is supplied, `STDIN` is used.

Example

```
(-t "/vmlinuz") ? print("-t /vmlinuz is tty\n") :
   print("-t /vmlinuz is not tty\n");
```

-u

Compliance

4 | 5 | NT

Syntax

Category `named unary operator (file test)`
Arguments `handle`

Arguments filename
Arguments none
Return Value 1 (true) '' (false)

Definition

The file test operator takes one file handle or filename as an argument. It returns 1 (true) if the file has the setuid bit set. It returns '' (false) if the files does not have the setuid bit set. In UNIX, setuid allows an executable to take on the UID of the user ownership of the executable itself while executing. All file test operators can take a special argument underscore, which means that the test is carried out on the same file handle as the last file test, stat(), or lstat() call. If no argument is supplied, $_ is used.

Example

```
(-u "/vmlinuz") ? print("-u /vmlinuz has suid
    set\n") :
   print("-u /vmlinuz does not have suid set\n");
```

-W

Compliance

4 | 5 | NT

Syntax

Category named unary operator (file test)
Arguments handle
Arguments filename
Arguments none
Return Value 1 (true) '' (false)

Definition

The file test operator takes one file handle or filename as an argument. It returns 1 (true) if the file is writable by the real UID/GID.

It returns '' (false) otherwise. For the superuser it always returns true. All file test operators can take a special argument underscore, which means that the test is carried out on the same file handle as the last file test, stat(), or lstat() call. If no argument is supplied, $_ is used.

Example

```
(-W "/vmlinuz") ? print("-W /vmlinuz is writable by
    real uid/gid\n") :
   print("-W /vmlinuz is not writable by real UID/
      GID\n");
```

-w

Compliance

4 **5** **NT**

Syntax

Category named unary operator (file test)
Arguments handle
Arguments filename
Arguments none
Return Value 1 (true) '' (false)

Definition

The file test operator takes one file handle or filename as an argument. It returns 1 (true) if the file is writable by the effective UID/GID. It returns '' (false) otherwise. For the superuser it always returns true. All file test operators can take a special argument underscore, which means that the test is carried out on the same file handle as the last file test, stat(), or lstat() call. If no argument is supplied, $_ is used.

Example

```
(-w "/vmlinuz") ? print("-w /vmlinuz is writable by
     effective uid/gid\n") :
    print("-1 /vmlinuz is not writable by
        effective uid/gid\n");
```

-X

Compliance

4 | 5 | NT

Syntax

Category named unary operator (file test)
Arguments handle
Arguments filename
Arguments none
Return Value 1 (true) '' (false)

Definition

The `file test` operator takes one file `handle` or `filename` as an argument. It returns `1` (true) if the file is executable by the real UID/GID. It returns `''` (false) otherwise. For the superuser it always returns true. All `file test` operators can take a special argument underscore, which means that the test is carried out on the same file `handle` as the last `file test`, `stat()`, or `lstat()` call. If no argument is supplied, `$_` is used.

Example

```
(-X _) ? print("-X /bin/ls is executable by real
    uid/gid\n") :
   print("-X /bin/ls is not executable by real
       uid/gid\n");
```

-X

Compliance

4 5 NT

Syntax

Category `named unary operator (file test)`
Arguments `handle`
Arguments `filename`
Arguments `none`
Return Value `1 (true) '' (false)`

Definition

The `file test` operator takes one file `handle` or `filename` as an argument. It returns `1` (true) if the file is executable by the effective UID/GID. It returns `''` (false) otherwise. For the superuser it always returns true. All `file test` operators can take a special argument underscore, which means that the test is carried out on the same file `handle` as the last `file test`, `stat()`, or `lstat()` call. If no argument is supplied, `$_` is used.

Example

```
(-x "/bin/ls") ? print("-x /bin/ls is executable by
     effective uid/gid\n") :
   print("-x /bin/ls is not executable by
       effective uid/gid\n");
```

-Z

Compliance

4 5 NT

Syntax

Category named unary operator (file test)
Arguments handle
Arguments filename
Arguments none
Return Value 1 (true) '' (false)

Definition

The file test operator takes one file handle or filename as an argument. It returns 1 (true) if the file has zero size. It returns '' (false) otherwise. All file test operators can take a special argument underscore, which means that the test is carried out on the same file handle as the last file test, stat() or lstat() call. If no argument is supplied, $_ is used.

Example

```
(-z "/vmlinuz") ? print("-z /vmlinuz has zero
size\n") :
   print("-z /vmlinuz does not have zero size\n");
```

abs

Compliance

5 **NT**

Syntax

Category named unary operator (numeric)
Arguments numeric value
Return Value numeric

Definition

This function returns the absolute value of its argument (it ignores any sign).

Example

```
print("abs(-10) = ",abs(-10),"\n");
```

accept

Compliance

[4] 5 NT

Syntax

Category `list operator (socket)`
Arguments `newsocket, genericsocket`
Return Value `integer (address of socket), '' (false)`

Definition

This function performs low-level UNIX socket call `accept()`.

alarm

Compliance

4 5

Syntax

Category `named unary operator (process)`
Arguments `integer (seconds)`
Return Value `integer (seconds to previous alarm)`

Definition

This function sets up a UNIX `SIGALRM` signal to be generated in the number of seconds specified. It is possible for Perl to trap such signals by calling specific signal handling subroutines, such as `trap()`.

Subseqent calls reset the `alarm()` time, retaining the number of seconds which were needed before the previous `SIGALRM` would have been generated. A call with zero seconds as an argument cancels the current `alarm()`.

Example

```
print("alarm(10) ",alarm(10),
" (to illustrate it needs to trapped c.f.
trap)\n");
```

atan2

Compliance

[4] 5 NT

Syntax

Category `list operator (numeric)`
Arguments `numeric, numeric`
Return Value `numeric`

Definition

The `atan2` function returns the arctangent of the arguments.

Example

```
print("atan2(60,2) = ",atan2(60,2),"\n");
```

bind

Compliance

[4] 5 NT

Syntax

Category `list operator (socket)`
Arguments `sockethandle, numeric (network address)`
Return Value `1 (true) '' (false)`

Definition

This function binds a network address to the socket handle, see the UNIX `bind()` call.

binmode

Compliance

4 5 NT

Syntax

Category `named unary operator (i/o)`
Arguments `handle`
Return Value `1 (success) or undefined (error)`

Definition

On systems that distinguish between text and binary files, this function forces binary mode treatment of the given file `handle`. In systems which do make the distinction, text files have the end of line characters (Carriage Return, Linefeed) automatically translated to the UNIX end of line character (Linefeed) when reading from the file (and vice versa when writing to the file); binary mode files do not have this automatic transformation.

Example

```
open(FIL,"file.dat");
binmode(FIL);
```

bless

Compliance

5 NT

Syntax

Category list operator (class)
Arguments variable
Arguments variable, classname
Return Value reference

Definition

This function assigns a class to the referenced object. This class is either explicitly stated in the call, or the name of the current package is used if a second argument is not used in the call. The reference is returned.

TIP Explictly state the class (use the two argument version of the call) if the code can be inherited by other classes because the class in the single argument call would not return the required value.

Example

```
$tmp = {};
bless $tmp, ATMPCLASS;
print "bless() \$tmp is now in class
",ref($tmp),"\n";
```

caller

Compliance

[4] 5 NT

Syntax

Category `named unary operator (scope)`
Arguments `expression`
Arguments `none`
Return Value `1 (true) '' (false)`
Return Value `(package, filename, line)`

Definition

This function is used to test the current scope of a subroutine call. If evaluated in a scalar context, it returns `1` or `''` depending on if the current code has been called as a subroutine (this includes code which is included using a `require()` or an `eval()` call). In an array context it supplies details of the calling context in a list comprising the `package` name, `filename`, and `line` of the call.

Example

```
sub testcaller {
    ($package, $file, $line) = caller;
}
&testcaller;
print "caller() Package=$package File=$file
Line=$line \n";
```

chdir

Compliance

4 **5** **NT**

Syntax

Category `named unary operator (files)`
Arguments `expression`
Arguments `none`
Return Value `1 (true) '' (false)`

Definition

This function changes the current directory to the directory specified. If no argument is given this call changes the current directory to be the home directory of the current user. It returns `1` upon success and `''` otherwise.

Example

```
chdir("/") ? print("It worked.\n") : print("It
    didn't work.\n");
```

chmod

Compliance

4 5

Syntax

Category `list operator (files)`
Arguments `list`
Return Value `numeric`

Definition

The first element in the list is the UNIX octal number representing the file permission. This function applies the mode specified by the octal number to all the files in the list that follows. It returns the number of files successfully modified.

Example

```
print "chmod() changed ",
chmod(0744,"/tmp/test1.txt","/tmp/test2.txt),"
      files.\n";
```

chomp

Compliance

5 NT

Syntax

Category `list operator (string)`
Arguments `list`
Arguments `variable`
Arguments `none`
Return Value `numeric`

Definition

This is an alternative to the `chop()` function. It removes characters at the end of strings corresponding to the `$INPUT_LINE_SEPARATOR` (`$/`). It returns the number of characters removed. It can be given a list of strings upon which to perform this operation. When given no arguments, the operation is performed on `$_`.

Example

```
$tmp="Aaagh!\n";
$ret = chomp $tmp;
print("chomp() ", $tmp, " returned ", $ret, "\n");
```

chop

Compliance

[4] 5 NT

Syntax

Category `list operator (string)`
Arguments `list`

Arguments variable
Arguments none
Return Value character

Definition

This function removes the last character of a string and returns that character. If given a list of arguments, the operation is performed on each one and the last character chopped is returned.

Example

```
$tmp = "1234";
$ret = chop $tmp;
print("chop() ", $tmp, " returned ", $ret, "\n");
```

TIP Use `chomp()` (with `$/` set to `"\n"`) rather than `chop()` if you are unsure that the string has a trailing newline because `chop()` will remove the last character regardless, but `chomp()` only removes it if it is a newline.

chown

Compliance

4 5 NT

Syntax

Category list operator (files)
Arguments list
Return Value numeric

Definition

This function changes the ownership of the specified files. The first two elements of the list define the user ID and the group ID to set this ownership; the subsequent items in the list are the file names that are changed. The return value is the number of files successfully changed.

Example

```
print("chown() ");
chown(1,1,"/tmp/test1.txt") ? print("Worked\n") :
print("Didn't work\n");
```

chr

Compliance

5 NT

Syntax

Category named unary operator (string)
Arguments numeric
Return Value character

Definition

This function returns the `character` indicated by the `numeric` argument.

Example

```
$E = chr(69);
print("chr() $E \n");
```

chroot

Compliance

4 5

Syntax

Category named unary operator (files)
Arguments directoryname

Arguments none
Return Value 1 (true) '' (false)

Definition

This function is equivalent to the UNIX `chroot()` function. Given a `directoryname`, this directory is treated as the root directory by all subsequent file system references, thus effectively hiding the rest of the file system outside the specified directory. This restriction applies to all subprocesses of the current process as well.

TIP Normal UNIX security limits this function to the superuser, and it is normally used to make processes safer by only allowing them access to the subdirectory tree relevant to their purpose.

Example

```
print("chroot() ");
chroot("/") ? print("Worked.\n") : print("Didn't
      work.\n");
```

close

Compliance

4 **5** **NT**

Syntax

Category named unary operator (files)
Arguments handle
Return Value 1 (true) '' (false)

Definition

This function closes the file opened with the file `handle`. This operation flushes all buffered output. If the file `handle` refers to a pipe, the Perl program waits until the process being piped has finished.

Example

```
open(INF,"/tmp/test1.txt");
$ret = close(INF);
print("close() Returned ",$ret," on success\n");
```

closedir

Compliance

4 5 NT

Syntax

Category named unary operator (file)
Arguments handle
Return Value 1 (true) '' (false)

Definition

This function closes the directory opened by `opendir()` by specifying the relevant directory `handle`.

Example

```
opendir(IND,"/tmp");
$ret = closedir(IND);
print("closedir() Returned ",$ret," on success\n");
```

connect

Compliance

4 5 NT

Syntax

Category `list operator (socket)`
Arguments `socket, name`
Return Value `1 (true) '' (false)`

Definition

This function is equivalent to the UNIX function call, which initiates a connection with a process, assuming that the process that is connected is waiting to accept.

continue

Compliance

4 5 NT

Syntax

Category `flow control`
Arguments `block`
Return Value `N/A`

Definition

A `continue` block is a syntax structure that allows a condition to be attached to another block (normally a `while` block). Any statements in the `continue` block are evaluated before the attached block is repeated.

Example

```
$i=0;
print "continue() ";
while ($i<10) {
      if ($i % 2)
         { print "${i}o "; next; }
```

```
        else
            {print "${i}e ";}
} continue {$i++}
print "\n";
```

cos

Compliance

4 5 NT

Syntax

Category `named unary operator (numeric)`
Arguments `expression`
Return Value `numeric`

Definition

This function returns the cosine value of the numeric `expression` supplied as an argument.

Example

```
print "cos() ",cos(60),"\n";
```

crypt

Compliance

4 5 NT

Syntax

Category `list operator`
Arguments `string, string`
Return Value `string`

Definition

This function is equivalent to the `crypt()` UNIX call (where available). It encrypts a `string` (the first argument) using a key (usually the first two letters of the first `string` itself) and returns the encrypted `string`.

Example

```
print "crypt() Password PA:
",crypt("Password","PA"),"\n";
```

dbmclose

Compliance

4 5

Syntax

Category `named unary operator (i/o)`
Arguments `arrayname`
Return Value `1 (true) '' (false)`

Definition

This function undoes the linking of an associative array to a DBM file (see `dbmopen()`).

NOTE This is depreciated in Perl 5, use `untie()` instead.

dbmopen

Compliance

[4] 5 NT

Syntax

Category `list operator (i/o)`
Arguments `arrayname, dbname, mode`
Return Value `fatal error if dbm not supported (Perl 4)`

Definition

This function links the associative array referred to by `arrayname`, to the DBM database (or equivalent) referred to by `dbname` (this name should not include the suffix). If the database does not exist, a new one with the specified mode will be opened (the mode being an octal `chmod()` style file protection).

NOTE This is depreciated in Perl 5, use `tie()` instead.

defined

Compliance

4 5 NT

Syntax

Category `named unary operator (misc)`
Arguments `expression`
Return Value `1 (true) '' (false)`

Definition

This function returns a Boolean value depending on whether the argument is defined or not. There is a subtle distinction between an undefined and a defined null value. Some functions return undefined null to indicate errors, while others return a defined null to indicate a particular result (use a comparison with the null string to test for this, rather than using `defined()`)

Example

```
@iexist = (1,2,3);
print("defined() The array \@iexist ");
defined @iexist ? print("exists.\n") : print("does
      not exist.\n");
```

delete

Compliance

4 5 NT

Syntax

Category `named unary operator (hash)`
Arguments `expression`
Return Value `value`

Definition

Use this function to delete an element from a hash array, given the key for the element to delete, returning the value of the deleted element.

Example

```
%Hash = (1, One, 2, Two, 3, Three);
print("delete() Deleted ",delete($Hash{1}),"\n");
```

die

Compliance

4 5 NT

Syntax

Category `list operator (i/o)`
Arguments `list`
Return Value `errorlevel`

Definition

This function terminates execution of the Perl script when called printing the value of the `list` argument to `STDERR` (as if called with `print(STDERR, list)`). The exit value is the current value of `$OS_ERROR ($!)`, which may have been set by a previous function. If this has a value of zero it returns `$CHILD_ERROR ($?)`. If this is zero, it exits with `errorlevel` 255. If the error message string specified by the list does not end in a newline, the text "`at $PROGRAM_NAME at line` *`line`*, where *`line`* is the line number of the Perl script.

Example

```
die("die() Now we can give an example of
 die()...exiting");
```

do

Compliance

4 **5** **NT**

Syntax

Category `(flow)`
Arguments `block`
Arguments `subroutine(list)`
Arguments `expression`
Return Value `special`

Definition

This is a syntax structure that allows repeated execution of a block of statements. The value returned is the result of the last statement in the block. Normally an exit condition is supplied after the `block`. The second form where the argument is `subroutine()` is a depreciated form. The third form executes the contents of the file name specified by the expression (but it is better to use `use()` or `require()` instead, because this has better error checking).

Example

```
$i=1;
print("do ");
$return = do {
  print $i, " ";
  $i++;
} until $i==3;
print("Returned $return\n");
```

dump

Compliance

4 5 NT

Syntax

Category `named unary operator (misc)`
Arguments `label`
Return Value `N/A`

Definition

This function causes the program to create a binary image core dump. This then allows the dumped image to be reloaded using the `undump()` function (if supported) which can effectively allow the use of precompiled Perl images. When reloaded, the program begins execution from the `label` specified. It is possible to set up a program which initializes data structures to `dump()` after the initialization so that execution is faster when reloading the dumped image.

each

Compliance

4 5 NT

Syntax

Category `named unary operator (hash)`
Arguments `variable`
Return Value `key, value`

Definition

This function allows iteration over the elements in an associative array. Each time it is evaluated, it returns another list of two elements (a `key`, value pair from the associative array). When all the elements have been returned, it returns a null list.

Example

```
%NumberWord = (1, One, 2, Two, 3, Three);
print("each() ");
while (($number,$wordform)=each(%NumberWord)) {
  print("$number:$wordform ");
}
print("\n");
```

endgrent

Compliance

4 5

Syntax

Category `(system files)`

Arguments none
Return Value 1 (true) '' (false)

Definition

This function closes the /etc/group file used by getgrent() and other group related functions. It is equivalent to the UNIX system call.

Example

```
($name,$pw,$gid,@members)=getgrent();
$returned = endgrent();
print("endgrent() Closes /etc/group [$name,$gid]",
    " file returning $returned.\n");
```

endhostent

Compliance

4 5

Syntax

Category (system files)
Arguments none
Return Value 1 (true) '' (false)

Definition

This function closes the TCP socket used by name server queries gethostbyname() and host related functions. It is equivalent to the UNIX system call.

Example

```
$host = gethostbyname("lynch");
$returned = endhostent();
print("endhostent() Closes /etc/hosts [$host]",
    " returning $returned.\n");
```

endnetent

Compliance

4 5

Syntax

Category (system files)
Arguments none
Return Value 1 (true) '' (false)

Definition

This function closes the /etc/networks file used by getnetent() and network related functions. This function is equivalent to the UNIX system call.

Example

```
($name,$alias,$net,$net) = getnetent();
$returned = endnetent();
print("endnetent() Closes /etc/networks [$name]",
    " returning $returned.\n");
```

endprotoent

Compliance

4 5

Syntax

Category (system files)
Arguments none
Return Value 1 (true) '' (false)

Definition

This function closes the `/etc/protocols` file used by `getprotoent()` and protocol related functions. It is equivalent to the UNIX system call.

Example

```
($name, $alias, $protocol) = getprotoent();
$returned = endprotoent();
print("endprotoent() Closes /etc/protocols ",
   "[$name,$alias,$protocol] file returning
$returned.\n");
```

endpwent

Compliance

4 5

Syntax

Category `(system files)`
Arguments `none`
Return Value `1 (true) '' (false)`

Definition

This function closes the `/etc/passwd` file used by `getpwent()` and password related functions. It is equivalent to the UNIX system call.

Example

```
($name,$pass,$uid,$gid,$quota,$name,$gcos,$logindir,$shell)
      = getpwent();
$returned = endpwent();
print("endpwent() Closes /etc/passwd
[$logindir,$shell] ",
   "file returning $returned.\n");
```

endservent

Compliance

4 5

Syntax

Category (system files)
Arguments none
Return Value 1 (true) '' (false)

Definition

This function closes the /etc/servers file used by getservent() and related functions. It is equivalent to the UNIX system call.

Example

```
($name,$aliases,$port,$protocol) = getservent();
$returned = endservent();
print("endservent() Closes /etc/servers [$name]",
    " file returning $returned.\n");
```

eof

Compliance

4 5 NT

Syntax

Category named unary operator (i/o)
Arguments handle
Arguments ()
Arguments none
Return Value 1 (true) '' (false)

Definition

This function tests if the file pointer to file specified by the file `handle` is at the and of the file. This is done by reading the next character and then undoing this operation (so is only suitable on files where this can be done safely). If no argument is supplied the file tested is the last file that was read. If the empty list is supplied then this tests if all the last file suppiled an argument to the Perl script are `eof()` (that is, it can be used as a termination condition in a `while` loop).

Example

```
open INF, "/tmp/test1.txt";
if (eof INF)
  {print "eof() TRUE\n";}
else
  {print "eof() FALSE\n";}
close INF;
```

eval

Compliance

4 5 NT

Syntax

Category `named unary operator (flow)`
Arguments `expression`
Arguments `block`
Arguments `none`
Return Value `special`

Definition

This function treats the expression like a Perl program and executes it returning the `return value` of the last statement executed. As the context of this execution is the same as that of the script itself, variable definitions and subroutine definitions persist. Syntax errors and runtime errors (including `die()`) are trapped and an undefined result is returned. If such an error does occur, `$EVAL_ERROR ($@)` is set. If no errors are found, `$@` is equal to a defined null string. If no expression is supplied, `$_` is the default argument. If the block syntax is used, the expressions in the block are evaluated only once within the script, which may be more efficient for certain situations.

TIP `eval()` traps possible error conditions that would otherwise crash a program. Therefore, it can be used to test if certain features are available that would cause runtime errors if used when not available.

Example

```
$ans = 3;
eval "$ans = ;";
if ($@ eq "")
  {print "eval() returned success.\n";}
else
  {print "eval() error: $@";}
```

exec

Compliance

4 **5** **NT**

Syntax

Category `list operator (process)`
Arguments `list`
Return Value `N/A`

Definition

This function passes control from the script to an external system command. There is no retain from this call so there is no return value. Note that `system()` calls external commands and does return to the next line in the calling Perl program.

This is equivalent to the UNIX system call `execvp()`.

Example

```
exec("cat /etc/motd");
```

exists

Compliance

5 NT

Syntax

Category `named unary operator (hash)`
Arguments `expression`
Return Value `1 (true) '' (false)`

Definition

This function tests if a given key value exists in an associative array, returning a Boolean value.

Example

```
%test = ( One, 1, Two, 2);
if (exists $test{One})
  {print "exists() returned success.\n";}
else
  {print "exists() returned an error.\n";}
```

exit

Compliance

4 5 NT

Syntax

Category `named unary operator (flow)`
Arguments `expression`
Arguments `none`
Return Value `value`

Definition

This function evaluates the expression given as an argument and exits the program with that error. The default value for the error is 0 if no argument is supplied. Note that `die()` allows an error message.

Example

```
exit(16);
```

exp

Compliance

4 5 NT

Syntax

Category `named unary operator (numeric)`
Arguments `expression`
Arguments `none`
Return Value `numeric`

Definition

This function returns the natural log base (`e`) to the power of `expression` (or of $_ if none specified).

Example

```
print "exp() e**1 is ",exp(1),"\n";
```

fcntl

Compliance

4 5

Syntax

Category `list operator (i/o)`
Arguments `handle, function, packed_parameters`

Definition

This function is equivalent to the UNIX `fnctl()` call. In Perl 5, use the `fntcl` module. In Perl 4, there should be some mechanism for linking the Perl functions to the system functions. This is usually executed when Perl is installed.

fileno

Compliance

4 5 NT

Syntax

Category `named unary operator (i/o)`
Arguments `handle`
Return Value `descriptor`

Definition

This function returns the file `descriptor` given a file `handle`.

Example

```
print("fileno() ",fileno(INF),"\n");
```

flock

Compliance

4 5 NT

Syntax

Category `list operator (i/o)`
Arguments `handle, operation`
Return Value `1 (true) '' (false)`

Definition

This calls the UNIX `flock()` function to access file locks. The `handle` is a Perl file `handle`. The operation is any valid `flock()` operation: place exclusive lock, place shared lock, and unlock. These operations are represented by numeric values.

fork

Compliance

4 5 NT

Syntax

Category `(process)`
Arguments `none`
Return Value `pid`

Definition

The `fork` function calls the UNIX `fork()` function or equivalent to fork a subprocess at this point. Returns the process ID (`pid`) of the child process to the calling process; returns 0 to the child process itself. The calling program should `wait()` on any child process it `forks` to avoid creating zombie processes.

Example

```
$pid = fork;
# Child only prints this
if ($pid != 0) {
  print("fork() Forking a process duplicates o/p:
$pid \n");
}
waitpid($pid,0);
# Child exits here
if ($$ != $origpid) { die; }
```

format

Compliance

4 5 NT

Syntax

Category `list operator (i/o)`
Arguments `format`

Definition

This function declares an output `format` specification. These formats are used in conjunction with the `write()` function to control the output of variables and text to conform to a standard layout structure. Normally, the specification includes some variables, specifying how many characters to output and whether to justify these left, right or centered. When `write()` is called, the actual values of the variables are used. This is useful for printing simple text reports and tables. The `format` specification itself is terminated by a period on a line by itself. The specification itself is in pairs of lines, the first describing the layout, and the second describing the variables to use in this layout.

Example

```
format STDOUT =
format() @>>>>>>> @>>>>>>> @>>>>>>>
         $t1,     $t2,      $t3
.
$t1 = One;
$t2 = Two;
$t3 = 3;
write;
```

formline

Compliance

5 NT

Syntax

Category `list operator (i/o)`
Arguments `picture, list`

Definition

This function is not usually called explictly (it is an implicit part of the `format` mechanism). It allows direct manipulation of the `format` process by adding values to the `format` accumulator (`$^A`).

Example

```
$tmp = formline <<'FINISH', Alpha, Beta, Gamma;
formline()  @>>>>>> @>>>>>> @>>>>>>
FINISH
print $^A;
```

getc

Compliance

4 5 NT

Syntax

Category `named unary operator (i/o)`
Arguments `handle`
Arguments `none`
Return Value `character`

Definition

This function returns the next character in specified file `handle`. The file defaults to `STDIN` if none is specified. If there are no more characters, null is returned.

Example

```
open INF, "/etc/motd";
print "getc() ",getc(INF),"\n";
close INF;
```

getgrent

Compliance

4 5

Syntax

Category `list operator (system files)`
Arguments `none`
Return Value `name`

Definition

This returns the next group name (or undefined) in the `/etc/group` system file. In a list context, it returns extra information taken from this file (or null list). This function is equivalent to the UNIX system call `getgrent()`.

Example

```
($name,$pw,$gid,@members)=getgrent();
print("getgrent() Examines /etc/group [$name,$gid]
file.\n");
```

getgrgid

Compliance

[4] 5

Syntax

Category `named unary operator (system files)`
Arguments `gid`
Return Value `name`

Definition

This function returns the next group name (or undefined) in the `/etc/group` system file with the supplied group ID (`gid`). In a list context, it returns extra information taken from this file (or null list). Equivalent to the UNIX system call `getgrgid()`.

Example

```
($grname,$grpw,$gid,@members) = getgrgid(0);
print("getgrgid() Returns group name given GID
[$grname]\n");
```

getgrname

Compliance

[4] 5

Syntax

Category `named unary operator (system files)`
Arguments `name`
Return Value `gid`

Definition

This function returns the next group ID, `gid`, (or undefined) in the `/etc/group` system file with the supplied group name. In a list context, it returns extra information taken from this file (or null list). It is equivalent to the UNIX system call `getgrname()`.

Example

```
($grname,$grpw,$gid,@members) = getgrnam("root");
print("getgrnam() Returns group GID given name
[$gid]\n");
```

gethostbyaddr

Compliance

[4] 5 NT

Syntax

Category `named unary operator (system files)`

Arguments address
Return Value name

Definition

It returns the host name, (or undefined) in the /etc/hosts system file (or via a Domain Name Server lookup) with the supplied host address. In a list context, The function returns extra information taken from this file (or null list). It is equivalent to the UNIX system call gethostbyaddr().

Example (Perl 5 only)

```
use Socket;
@a=(140,203,7,103);
$addr=pack('C4',@a);
($name,$alias,$adrtype,$length,@address)=gethostbyaddr($addr,AF_INET);
print("gethostbyaddr() [$alias].\n");
```

gethostbyname

Compliance

[4] 5 NT

Syntax

Category named unary operator (system files)
Arguments name
Return Value address

Definition

This function returns the host address, (or undefined) in the /etc/hosts system file (or via a Domain Name Server lookup) with the supplied host name. In a list context, it returns extra information taken from this file (or null list). This function is equivalent to the UNIX system call gethostbyname().

Example

```
($name,$alias,$adrtype,$length,@address)=gethostbyname("lynch");
print("gethostbyname() [$alias].\n");
```

gethostent

Compliance

4 5 NT

Syntax

Category `(system files)`
Arguments `none`
Return Value `name`

Definition

`gethostent` returns the next host `name`, (or undefined) in the `/etc/hosts` system file (or via a Domain Name Server lookup). In a list context, it returns extra information taken from this file (or null list). This function is equivalent to the UNIX system call `gethostent()`.

Example

```
($name,$alias,$adrtype,$length,@address)=gethostbyname("lynch");
print("gethostent() [$alias].\n");
```

getlogin

Compliance

4 5

Syntax

Category (system files)
Arguments none
Return Value name

Definition

This function returns the current login name from the `/etc/utmp` system file.

Example

```
print ("getlogin() ",getlogin(),"\n");
```

getnetbyaddr

Compliance

[4] 5

Syntax

Category (system files)
Arguments address
Return Value name

Definition

`getnetbyaddr` returns the network `name` from the `/etc/networks` system file given a network `address`. In a list context, it returns extra information from this file. This function is equivalent to UNIX's `getnetbyaddr()` call.

Example

```
($name,$alias,$addrtype,$net) = getnetent();
($name,$alias,$addrtype,$net) =
getnetbyaddr($net,$addrtype);
print("getnetbyaddr() Reads /etc/networks
[$name]\n");
```

getnetbyname

Compliance

[4] 5

Syntax

Category named unary operator (system files)
Arguments name
Return Value address

Definition

Returns the network address from the /etc/networks system file, given a network name. In a list context returns extra information from this file. Equivalent to the UNIX getnetbyname() call.

Example

```
($name,$alias,$addrtype,$net) =
getnetbyname("localnet");
print("getnetbyname() Reads /etc/networks
[$name]\n");
```

getnetent

Compliance

4 5

Syntax

Category (system files)
Arguments none
Return Value name

Definition

This function returns the next network name from the /etc/networks system file. In a list context, it returns extra information from this file. getnetent is equivalent to the UNIX getnetent() call.

Example

```
($name,$alias,$addrtype,$net) = getnetent();
print("getnetent() Reads /etc/networks
[$name,$addrtype]\n");
```

getpeername

Compliance

[4] 5 NT

Syntax

Category named unary operator (socket)
Arguments socket
Return Value name

Definition

getpeername is equivalent to the UNIX system getpeername() system call.

getpgrp

Compliance

4 5

Syntax

Category `named unary operator (process)`
Arguments `pid`
Return Value `gid`

Definition

This function returns the group ID (`gid`) of the process with the process ID (`pid`).

Example

```
print("getpgrp() ",getpgrp(0),"\n");
```

getppid

Compliance

4 5

Syntax

Category `(process)`
Arguments `none`
Return Value `pid`

Definition

`getppid` returns the process ID (`pid`) of the parent process of the current process.

Example

```
print("getppid() ",getppid(),"\n");
```

getpriority

Compliance

[4] 5

Syntax

Category `list operator (process)`
Arguments `type, id`
Return Value `priority`

Definition

This function calls the UNIX `getpriority()` function. The type is one of `PRIO_PROCESS`, `PRIO_PGGRP`, and `PRIO_USER`. The `id` is the relevant ID for this (`pid` for `PRIO_PROCESS`, `pid` for `PRIO_PGGRP`, `uid` for `PRIO_USER`). If zero is used as the `id`, the current process, process group, or user is used.

Example

```
print("getpriority() ",getpriority(0,0),"\n");
```

getprotobyname

Compliance

[4] 5

Syntax

Category `named unary operator (system files)`
Arguments `name`
Return Value `protocol`

Definition

This function returns the protocol number from the /etc/protocols system file, given the protocol name. In a list context, it returns extra information from this file. getprotobyname is equivalent to the UNIX getprotobyname() call.

Example

```
($name, $alias, $protocol) = getprotobyname("IP");
print("getprotobyname() /etc/protocols
[$name,$alias,$protocol].\n");
```

getprotobynumber

Compliance

[4] 5

Syntax

Category named unary operator (system files)
Arguments protocol
Return Value name

Definition

This function returns the protocol name from the /etc/protocols system file, given the protocol number. In a list context, it returns extra information from this file. getprotobynumber is equivalent to the UNIX getprotobynumber() call.

Example

```
($name, $alias, $protocol) = getprotobynumber(0);
print("getprotobynumber() /etc/protocols
[$name,$alias,$protocol].\n");
```

getprotoent

Compliance

4 5

Syntax

Category `(system files)`
Arguments `none`
Return Value `name`

Definition

This returns the next protocol name from the `/etc/protocols` system file. In a list context, it returns extra information from this file. This function is equivalent to UNIX's `getprotoent()` call.

Example

```
($name, $alias, $protocol) = getprotoent();
print("getprotoent() Closes /etc/protocols
[$name,$alias,$protocol].\n");
```

getpwent

Compliance

4 5

Syntax

Category `(system files)`
Arguments `none`
Return Value `name`

Definition

`getpwent` returns the user `name` from the next entry in the `/etc/passwd` system file. In a list context, it returns extra information from this file. This function is equivalent to the UNIX `getpwent()` call.

Example

```
($name,$pass,$uid,$gid,$quota,$name,$gcos,$logindir,$shell)
= getpwent();
print("getpwent() /etc/passwd
[$logindir,$shell].\n");
```

getpwnam

Compliance

[4] 5

Syntax

Category `named unary operator (system files)`
Arguments `name`
Return Value `uid`

Definition

This function returns the user ID (`uid`) from the `/etc/passwd` system file given the user `name`. In a list context, it returns extra information from this file. It is equivalent to the UNIX `getpwnam()` call.

Example

```
($name,$pass,$uid,$gid,$quota,$name,$gcos,$logindir,$shell)
   = getpwnam("root");
print("getpwnam() /etc/passwd
[$logindir,$shell].\n");
```

getpwuid

Compliance

[4] 5

Syntax

Category named unary operator (system files)
Arguments uid
Return Value name

Definition

`getpwiud` returns the user `name` from the `/etc/passwd` system file given the user ID (`uid`). In a list context, `getpwuid` returns extra information from this file. This function is equivalent to the UNIX `getpwnam()` call.

Example

```
($name,$pass,$uid,$gid,$quota,$name,$gcos,$logindir,$shell)
    = getpwuid(0);
print("getpwuid() /etc/passwd
[$logindir,$shell].\n");
```

getservbyname

Compliance

[4] 5

Syntax

Category list operator (system files)
Arguments name, protocol
Return Value port

Definition

`getservbyname` returns the port number of the service from the `/etc/services` system file given the `service name` and the `protocol name`. In a list context, it returns extra information from this file. This function is equivalent to UNIX's `getservbyname()` call.

Example

```
($name,$aliases,$port,$protocol) =
getservbyname("tcpmux","tcp");
print("getservbyname() /etc/servers [$name].\n");
```

getservbyport

Compliance

[4] 5

Syntax

Category `list operator (system files)`
Arguments `port, protocol`
Return Value `name`

Definition

`getservbyport` returns the service name of the service from the `/etc/services` system file given the `port number` and the protocol `name`. In a list context, it returns extra information from this file. It is equivalent to the UNIX `getservbyport()` call.

Example

```
($name,$aliases,$port,$protocol) =
getservbyport(512,"tcp");
print("getservbyport() Problem with this!
[$name]\n");
```

getservent

Compliance

4 5

Syntax

Category `(system files)`
Arguments `none`
Return Value `name`

Definition

This function returns the next service name of the service from the `/etc/services` system file. In a list context, it returns extra information from this file. It is equivalent to the UNIX `getservet()` call.

Example

```
($name,$aliases,$port,$protocol) = getservent();
print("getservent() /etc/servers [$name].\n");
```

getsockname

Compliance

[4] 5 NT

Syntax

Category `named unary operator (socket)`
Arguments `socket`
Return Value `address`

Definition

This function returns the address of the socket.

getsockopt

Compliance

4 5 NT

Syntax

Category `list operator (socket)`
Arguments `socket, level, optionname`
Return Value `option`

Definition

This function is equivalent to the UNIX `getsockopt()` system call and returns the socket option requested. However, if an error has happened, the function's return is undefined.

glob

Compliance

5 NT

Syntax

Category `named unary operator (files)`
Arguments `expression`
Return Value `list`

Definition

This function returns the `list` of files resulting from expanding the expression with any wildcards. This is equivalent to `<*.*>`.

Example

```
@files = glob("/tmp/*.txt");
print "glob() ",$files[1],"\n";
```

gmtime

Compliance

4 5 NT

Syntax

Category `named unary operator (time)`
Arguments `expression`
Arguments `none`
Return Value `list`

Definition

Given a time as an argument (measured in seconds since 1 Jan. 1970), `gmtime` returns a `list` of nine elements with that time broken down into seconds, minutes, hours, day of month, month, year, day of week, day of year, daylight saving enabled (daylight saving enabled is either `1` for on or `0` for off). If no argument is used, the current time is reported. If the system supports POSIX time zones, the time returned is localized for the Greenwich Mean Time.

In a scalar context, the `ctime()` style output (a string describing the time in readable form) is returned.

Example

```
($sec,$min,$hour,$mday,$mon,$year,$wday,$ydat,$isdst)
= gmtime();
print "gmtime() 19$year-$mon-$mday\n";
```

goto

Compliance

4 5 NT

Syntax

Category (flow)
Arguments label
Arguments expression
Arguments &name
Return Value N/A

Definition

The first form transfers control flow in the program to the specified `label`. The second allows the evaluation of an `expression` to supply the label name to transfer control to. The third form is a way of passing control from one subroutine to another subroutine so that, to the original caller, it appears that the second subroutine was called directly.

Example

```
print "goto ";
$count = 1;
TESTGOTO: {
   print $count, " ";
   $label = "TESTGOTO";
   if ($count < 2) {
    $count++;
    goto $label;
   }
   else {
    goto FINISH;}
}
FINISH: print "\n";
```

grep

Compliance

4 5 NT

Syntax

Category `list operator (lists)`
Arguments `expression, list`
Arguments `block, list`
Return Value `list`

Definition

This function evaluates the `expression` or `block` for each of the elements in the supplied list, returning a list of the elements that were evaulated as true. The most common use for this is with a pattern match operation as the expression, and a list of strings to be processed.

Example

```
@a = ("One","Two","Three","Four","Five");
print("grep(), ",grep(/^T.*/,@a), "\n");
```

hex

Compliance

4 5 NT

Syntax

Category `named unary operator (numeric)`
Arguments `expression`
Return Value `numeric`

Definition

This function evaluates the expression as a hexadecimal string and returns the decimal equivalent.

Example

```
print("hex() ",hex("ff"), "\n");
```

import

Compliance

5 NT

Syntax

Category `list operator (scope)`
Arguments `list`
Return Value `1 (true) '' (false)`

Definition

In the Perl 5 module system, each module has a local `import()` method. This is called when `use()` includes modules.

index

Compliance

[4] 5 NT

Syntax

Category `list operator (string)`
Arguments `string substring`

Arguments `string substring position`
Return Value `position`

Definition

`index` returns the position in the supplied string where the `substring` first occurs. If a position is supplied as an argument, the search begins at this element (thus repeated calls can find all occurrences if the found position is passed back as the argument to the subsequent calls). If the `substring` is not found, the return value is `-1`. All array element numbers are based on `$[`, which is normally set to zero. If this value is altered it will change the way `index()` works. This is because index will start its search from `$[` if no position argument is supplied, and it will return `$[-1` when there is no match found.

Example

```
$ans1 = index("abcdefghijiklmdef:-)","def");
$ans2 = index("abcdefghijiklmdef","def",$ans1+3);
print("index() def is at $ans1 and next at
$ans2\n");
```

int

Compliance

4 **5** **NT**

Syntax

Category `named unary operator (numeric)`
Arguments `expression`
Arguments `none`
Return Value `integer`

Definition

This function returns the integer part of the expression. It uses `$_` as the argument if none is specified.

Example

```
print("int() ",int(345.678), "\n");
```

ioctl

Compliance

[4] 5

Syntax

Category `list operator (files)`
Arguments `handle, function, parameter`
Return Value `numeric`

Definition

This function calls the UNIX `ioctl()` function with the specified packed parameter. It returns undefined if the operating system returns `-1`. It returns the string `0 but true` if the operating system returns `0`. Otherwise, it returns the value returned by the operating system.

join

Compliance

[4] 5 NT

Syntax

Category `list operator (lists)`
Arguments `expression, list`
Return Value `string`

Definition

This function returns the string comprising each element in the list joined with the string expression.

Example

```
@listone = (0, 1, 2, 3);
print("join() ",join("-",@listone),"\n");
```

keys

Compliance

4 5 NT

Syntax

Category named unary operator (hash)
Arguments array
Return Value list

Definition

This function returns a list comprising each key in the associative array passed as a parameter. In a scalar context, the number of keys is returned. The returned list is ordered by the internal storage requirements, so it is often useful to sort this array before processing.

Example

```
%assocone = (
    One, 1,
    Two, 2,
    Three, 3,
    Four, 4
    );
print("keys() ",join("-",keys(%assocone)),"\n");
```

kill

Compliance

4 5

Syntax

Category `list operator (process)`
Arguments `signal, list`
Return Value `1 (true) '' (false)`

Definition

This function kills the processes with the PIDs in the supplied list by sending the signal level specified. If the signal level is negative, the process groups are killed.

last

Compliance

4 5 NT

Syntax

Category `(flow)`
Arguments `label`
Arguments `none`
Return Value `N/A`

Definition

This causes control to exit the loop specified by `label` (or the innermost loop if none is specified).

Example

```
i=1;
print("last() ");
loop: while (I<10) {
   last loop if i=3;
   print(i);
}
print("\n");
```

lc

Compliance

5 NT

Syntax

Category named unary operator (string)
Arguments expression
Return Value string

Definition

This function returns the lowercase version of any supplied expression.

Example

```
print"lc() ",lc("ABCDef"), "\n";
```

lcfirst

Compliance

5 NT

Syntax

Category named unary operator (string)
Arguments expression
Return Value string

Definition

This function returns the `string` with the first character of the expression lowercased.

Example

```
print"lcfirst() ",lcfisrt("ABCDef"), "\n";
```

length

Compliance

4 5 NT

Syntax

Category named unary operator (string)
Arguments expression
Arguments none
Return Value numeric

Definition

`length` returns the length of the string specified by expression. If no expression is supplied, `$_` is evaluated.

Example

```
print("length() ",length("01234"),"\n");
```

link

Compliance

[4] 5

Syntax

Category `list operator (files)`
Arguments `filename, linkname`
Return Value `numeric`

Definition

This function creates a new link named after the second argument linking to the `filename` specified in the first argument; returns `1` or `0` for success or failure.

Example

```
$result = link("/usr/local",:"/tmp/link");
print("link() $result\n");
```

listen

Compliance

[4] 5 NT

Syntax

Category `list operator (socket)`
Arguments `socket, queuesize`
Return Value `1 (true) '' (false)`

Definition

This is equivalent to the UNIX `listen()` system call. If you are using `accepts` on a socket, `listen` tells the system that it is available.

local

Compliance

[4] 5 NT

Syntax

Category `named unary operator (scope)`
Arguments `expression`
Return Value `N/A`

Definition

Modifies all the variables listed to be local to the current block. If there is more than one element, the list must be enclosed in parentheses. Any errors would be syntax errors. Although `local()` does prevent pollution of the global namespace with variables in subroutines, `my()` is safer than `local()` because it also creates new copies of the variables for each recursive call of a subroutine.

localtime

Compliance

4 5 NT

Syntax

Category `named unary operator (time)`
Arguments `expression`

Arguments none
Return Value list

Definition

Given a time as an argument (measured in seconds since 1 Jan. 1970), this function returns a list of nine elements with that time broken down into seconds, minutes, hours, day of month, month, year, day of week, day of year, daylight saving enabled (daylight saving enabled is either `1` for on or `0` for off). If no argument is used, the current time is reported. If the system supports POSIX time zones, the time returned is localized for the current time zone.

In a scalar context, the `ctime()` style output is returned (a string describing the time in readable form).

Example

```
($sec,$min,$hour,$mday,$mon,$year,$wday,$ydat,$isdst)
= localtime();
print "localtime() 19$year-$mon-$mday\n";
```

log

Compliance

4 5 NT

Syntax

Category named unary operator (numeric)
Arguments expression
Arguments none
Return Value numeric

Definition

This returns the logarithm (using the natural logarithm base) of the `expression` (or of `$_` if none specified).

Example

```
print("log() ",log(2.5),"\n");
```

lstat

Compliance

[4] 5

Syntax

Category `named unary operator (files)`
Arguments `handle`
Arguments `expression`
Return Value `list`

Definition

The `lstat` function returns the file statistics of the file pointed to by the file `handle` (or a file `handle` produced by evaluating the expression). This is equivalent to `stat()`, but if the file is a symbolic link, the statistics are generated for the symbolic link itself rather than the file being linked to. Note that, like the `file test` operators, `lstat()` can take a special argument underscore, which means that the test is carried out on the same file `handle` as the last `file test`, `stat()`, or `lstat()` call.

Example

```
($device,$inode,$mode,$nlink,$uid,$gid,$rdev,$size,
$atime,$mtime,$ctime,$blksize,$blocks) = lstat("/
tmp/link");
print("lstat() $device, $inode, $ctime \n");
```

m//

Compliance

4 5 NT

Syntax

Category named unary operator (pattern)
Arguments m/<pattern>/<optionlist>
Arguments /<pattern>/<optionlist>
Return Value 1 (true) '' (false)

Definition

This function searches the default string for the pattern using regular expression pattern matching. It returns 1 if a match is found. Otherwise, '' is returned. The default string can be assigned to the match using either the =~ or !~ operators; otherwise, it is $_.

Example

```
$_ = "Happy MaN";
print "m// ",/n$/i,"\n";
```

map

Compliance

5 NT

Syntax

Category list operator (list)
Arguments block list
Arguments expression, list
Return Value list

Definition

This function evaluates the specified expression (or block) for each individual member of the specified list. This is done by assigning `$_` to each member of the list and evaluating the `expression` (or `block`). The value returned is the `list` of all these results (not necessarily one Perl element of the list).

Example

```
@result = map($_+1,(0,1,2));
print("map() ",@result,."\n");
```

mkdir

Compliance

[4] 5 NT

Syntax

Category `list operator (files)`
Arguments `filename, mode`
Return Value `1 or 0`

Definition

The `mkdir` function creates a directory with a name specified by the `filename`, with the `mode` specified by the octal mode. If it fails, `$OS_ERROR` (`$!`) is set to operating system error.

Example

```
print("mkdir() ",mkdir("/tmp/testdir",0777), "\n");
```

msgctl

Compliance

[4] 5

Syntax

Category `list operator (System V)`
Arguments `id, cmd, arg`
Return Value `special`

Definition

This function is equivalent to the UNIX system call `msgctl()`, if supported, and provides a variety of message control operations as specified by CMD.

msgget

Compliance

[4] 5

Syntax

Category `list operator (System V)`
Arguments `key, flags`
Return Value `special`

Definition

This function is equivalent to the UNIX system call `msgget()`, if supported, and returns the message queue identifier associated with key.

msgrcv

Compliance

[4] 5

Syntax

Category `list operator (System V)`
Arguments `id, var.size, type, flags`
Return Value `special`

Definition

This is equivalent to the UNIX system call `msgrcv()`, if supported. This function reads a message from the queue associated with the message queue identifier, specified by `msqid`, and places it in the structure pointed to by `msgp`.

msgsnd

Compliance

[4] 5

Syntax

Category `list operator (System V)`
Arguments `id, msg, flags`
Return Value `special`

Definition

The `msgsnd` function is equivalent to the UNIX system call `msgsnd()`, if supported, and sends a message to the queue associated with the message queue identifier.

my

Compliance

5 NT

Syntax

Category `named unary operator (scope)`
Arguments `expression`
Return Value `N/A`

Definition

This function declares each of the variables listed to be `local()` to the `block`. If more than one variable is specified, parentheses are required. The `my()` specification is stronger than the the `local()` specification because it not only stops pollution of the global namespace but also creates a stack frame for subroutine calls so that recursive calls will behave as one would expect with local variables.

next

Compliance

4 5 NT

Syntax

Category `named unary operator (flow)`
Arguments `label`
Arguments `none`
Return Value `N/A`

Definition

This operator allows branching within a loop so that the execution skips onto the next instance of the loop.

Example

```
print("next ");
@array = ("a","b","c");
loop: foreach $elem (@array) {
   next if $elem =~ /^a/;
   print $elem;
}
print "\n";
```

no

Compliance

5 NT

Syntax

Category `list operator (module)`
Arguments `module, list`
Return Value `N/A`

Definition

Using this function, particularly useful when using pragmas, is the reverse of `use()`.

Example

```
use integer;
# code using integer arithmetic here
no integer;
# back to floating point arithmetic
```

oct

Compliance

4 5 NT

Syntax

Category `named unary operator (numeric)`
Arguments `expression`
Return Value `numeric`

Definition

This function evaluates the expression as an octal string and returns the decimal value.

Example

```
print("oct() ",oct("88"), "\n");
```

open

Compliance

[4] 5 NT

Syntax

Category `list operator (files)`
Arguments `handle, filename`
Arguments `handle`
Return Value `TRUE (non zero) or FALSE (undefined)`

Definition

This function opens a file using the specified file `handle`. The file `handle` may be an expression; the resulting value is used as the `handle`. If no `filename` is specified, a variable with the same name as the file `handle` is used (this should be a scalar variable with a string value referring to the `filename`).

The `filename` string may be prefixed with the following values to indicate the mode:

- < Read, this is the default.
- > Write.
- +> Read/write—starting with new file.
- +< Read/write using existing file.
- >> Append.
- `<command> |` Input pipe; the file name is actually a subshell command from which the file handle is piped.
- `| <command>` Output pipe; the file name is actually a subshell command to which the output of the file handle is piped.

The special file name - can refer to either `STDIN` (-) when reading) or `STDOUT` (>-), when writing.

Example

```
open(FIL,"/tmp/notexist") ||
   print("open() failed as file did not
exist.\n");
```

opendir

Compliance

[4] 5 NT

Syntax

Category `list operator (files)`
Arguments `handle, dirname`
Return Value `1 (true) '' (false)`

Definition

Opens a directory `handle` for the directory name specified. If the `dirname` is an expression this can be evaluated to return a name.

Example

```
opendir (DIR, "/tmp/notexist") ||
   print("opendir() diled as directory dod not
exist.\n");
```

ord

Compliance

4 5 NT

Syntax

Category `named unary operator (string)`
Arguments `expression`
Arguments `none`
Return Value `numeric`

Definition

This function returns the numeric ASCII code of the first character in the expression (or $_ if none specified).

Example

```
print("ord() ",ord("A"), "\n");
```

pack

Compliance

[4] 5 NT

Syntax

Category `list operator (records)`
Arguments `template, list`
Return Value `string`

Definition

This function returns a packed version of the data in the list using the template to determine how it is coded. The template comprises a sequence of characters, each specifying the data type of the matching data item in the list.

Character	Description
@	Null fill to absolute position
A	ASCII string with spaces to pad
a	ASCII string with nulls to pad
b	Bit string (ascending bit order)
B	Bit string (descending bit order)
c	Signed char value
C	Unsigned char value
d	Double-precision float in the native format
f	Single-precision float in the native format
h	Hex string (low nybble first)
H	Hex string (high nybble first)
i	Signed integer value
I	Unsigned integer value
l	Signed long integer value
L	Unsigned long integer value

continued

continued

Character	Description
n	Short integer "network" order
N	Long integer "network" order
p	Pointer to a null-terminated string
P	Pointer to a structure (fixed-length string)
s	Signed short integer value
S	Unsigned short integer value
u	UUencoded string
v	Short integer "VAX" (little-endian) order
V	Long integer "VAX" (little-endian) order
x	Null byte
X	Back up a byte

A concise form of template can be used by appending a number after any letter to repeat that format specifier. For `aA`, the number uses one value and pads the rest. For `bB`, the number indicates the number of bits. For `hH`, the number indicates the number of nybbles. For `P`, the number indicates the size of the pointer structure. Using an asterisk in place of a number means to repeat the format specifier as necessary to use up all list values. Note that some packed structures may not be portable across machines (in particular, network and floating point formats). It should be possible to unpack the data using the same format specification with an `unpack()` call.

Example

```
Use Socketl
@a=(140,203,7,103);
$addr=pack('C4',@a);
($name,$alias,$adrtype,$length,@address)=gethostbyaddr
($addr,AF_INET);print("pack() ",@a, "packed as:
$addr".\n");
```

package

Compliance

4 5 NT

Syntax

Category `named unary operator (class)`
Arguments `name`
Return Value `N/A`

Definition

Calling this function declares that all unqualified dynamic variables in the current block are in the scope of the specified package name. This is normally done in the header of a file to be included as a package or a module in other programs that `require()` or `use()`. Note that this does apply to variables declared as `local()` but not to variables declared as `my()`.

pipe

Compliance

[4] 5

Syntax

Category `list operator (process)`
Arguments `readhandle, writehandle`
Return Value `1 (true) '' (false)`

Definition

Links named pipes like the UNIX function `pipe()`.

pop

Compliance

4 5 NT

Syntax

Category `name unary operator (array)`
Arguments `variable`
Return Value `value`

Definition

This function removes the top item from the array specified and returns that element.

Example

```
@a = (1,2,3,4);
print("pop() ",pop(@a), "leaves ",@a,"\n");
```

pos

Compliance

5 NT

Syntax

Category `named unary operator (pattern)`
Arguments `variable`
Return Value `numeric`

Definition

Returns the offset that the last pattern match (`m//g`) reached when searching the scalar variable specified as an argument. It can be assigned to alter the bahavior of the next match.

Example

```
$name = "alpha1 alpha2 alpha3 alpha4";
$name =~ m/alpha/g;
print("pos() ", pos($name), "\n");
```

print

Compliance

4 5 NT

Syntax

Category `list operator (i/o)`
Arguments `handle, list`
Arguments `list`
Arguments `none`
Return Value `1 (true) '' (false)`

Definition

Prints the list to the file represented by the file `handle`. If no file `handle` is specified the default file `handle` is `STDOUT`. This default file handle may be altered using the `select()` operator. If no list argument is specified, `$_` is printed.

Example

```
$return = print "print() ";
print "returns $return on success.\n");
```

printf

Compliance

4 5 NT

Syntax

Category `list operator (i/o)`
Arguments `filehandle list`
Arguments `list`
Return Value `1 (true) '' (false)`

Definition

This function uses the C `printf` format specifiers to control the printed output. It is equivalent to

```
print filehandle, sprintf(list);
```

As with `print()` the default file handle is `STDOUT`.

Example

```
printf("printf() An integer printed with leading
zeroes %05d.\n",9);
```

push

Compliance

[4] 5 NT

Syntax

Category `list operator (array)`
Arguments `array, list`
Return Value `numeric`

Definition

This appends the elements in the specified `list` on the end of the specified `array` and returns the new number of elements in the list.

Example

```
@a = (1);
$num = push(@a,2,3,4,5);
print("push() Added ",$num-1," elements to array:",
@a,"\n");
```

q/STRING/

Compliance

4 5 NT

Syntax

Category `(string)`
Arguments `q/string/`
Return Value `value`

Definition

This is a standard quote used to surpress special interpretation of characters giving a literal string. You can use single quotes `'string'` or the letter `q` with delimiters. Any delimiter will do as long as it is not used in the string. The backslash character can be used to escape any reference to the delimiting character itself in the string.

Example

```
print(q!q// The only special character is the
delimiter itself \!!, "\n");
```

qq/STRING/

Compliance

4 5 NT

Syntax

Category `(string)`
Arguments `qq/string/`
Return Value `value`

Definition

This is a double quote, used to allow interpolation of special characters within the string as required. You can use double quote `"string"` or the double `qq` with delimiters. The backslash character can be used to disable the special meaning of interpolated characters, including the delimiter itself.

Example

```
$newline = "\n";
print(qq!qq// double quoted with interpolation!
$newline!);
```

quotemeta

Compliance

5 NT

Syntax

Category `named unary operator (pattern)`
Arguments `expression`
Return Value `string`

Definition

`quotemeta` returns the value of the expression with all the metacharacters backslashed.

Example

```
print(quotemeta("quotameta() I can use any
metcharacter $ \ "),"\n");
```

qw/STRING/

Compliance

5 NT

Syntax

Category `(list)`
Arguments `qw/string/`
Return Value `list`

Definition

This function returns a list of words in string. Spaces are used as delimiters in the string to produce this list.

Example

```
print("qw// ",qw("1 2 3 4 5"),"\n");
```

qx/STRING/

Compliance

4 5 NT

Syntax

Category `(process)`
Arguments `qx/string/`
Return Value `special`

Definition

This is a back quote, used to allow interpolation of special characters within the string as required and then execute the resulting command as a system command. You can use back quotes `'string'` or the letters `qx` with delimiters. The backslash character can be used to disable the special meaning of interpolated characters, including the delimiter itself. The return value is the return value of the `system()` call.

Example

```
print("qx// ",qx!du -s /tmp!);
```

rand

Compliance

[4] [5] [NT]

Syntax

Category `named unary operator (numeric)`
Arguments `expression`
Arguments `none`
Return Value `numeric`

Definition

This function returns a real number between `0` and the number evaluated as expression (the upper limit is `1` if no expression is specified). The upper limit must be positive. As the function calls a pseudorandom generator, it should be possible to generate the same sequence of numbers repeatedly unless the initial seed value is altered with `srand()`.

Example

```
print("rand(), ",rand,"\n");
```

read

Compliance

[[4]] [5] [NT]

Syntax

Category `list operator (i/o)`
Arguments `handle, variable, length, offset`
Arguments `handle, variable, length`
Return Value `1 (true) '' (false)`

Definition

Reads length bytes from file `handle` into variable (starting at offset if specified). It returns the number of bytes actually read.

Example

```
open(INF,"/etc/services") || die "Error reading
file, stopped";
read(INF,$result,10);
print("read() $result \n");
close(INF)
```

readdir

Compliance

4 5 NT

Syntax

Category `list operator (i/o)`
Arguments `dirhandle`
Return Value `lname`

Definition

In a list context, this function returns a list of the files in the directory specified by the directory `handle`. In a scalar context, it returns the next file name in the directory.

Example

```
opendir(DIR,"/tmp");
@file = readdir(DIR);
print("readdir() ",@files, "\n");
```

readlink

Compliance

4 5

Syntax

Category `named unary operator (files)`
Arguments `expression`
Arguments `none`
Return Value `value`

Definition

This function returns the value of the symbolic link specified by `expression` (or `$_` if none specified). If symbolic links are not implemented, it gives a fatal error. If symbolic links are supported, but there is some system error, the error is returned in `$OS_ERROR` (`$!`).

recv

Compliance

[4] 5 NT

Syntax

Category `list operator (socket)`
Arguments `socket, variable, length, flags`
Return Value `address`

Definition

The `recv` function is equivalent to UNIX system call `recv()` and receives a message on a socket.

redo

Compliance

4 5 NT

Syntax

Category `(flow)`
Arguments `label`
Arguments `none`
Return Value `N/A`

Definition

This function passes control directly to the `label` without executing any continue block. If no `label` is specified, the innermost loop is used.

ref

Compliance

5 NT

Syntax

Category `named unary operator (class)`
Arguments `expression`
Return Value `package`

Definition

This function returns the package of a `bless()ed` variable, `TRUE` if the variable is a reference, or `FALSE`. The return value for `TRUE` is actually the type of the variable (for example `ARRAY`, `HASH`, `REF`, `SCALAR`).

Example

```
$tmp = {};
bless $tmp, ATMPCLASS;
print "ref() \$tmp is now in class
",ref($tmp),"\n";
```

rename

Compliance

4 5 NT

Syntax

Category `list operator (files)`
Arguments `oldname, newname`
Return Value `1 (true) 0 (fail)`

Definition

This function renames files on the same file system from `oldname` to `newname`.

Example

```
$returned = rename("/tmp/test","/tmp/test2");
print("rename() returned $returned \n");
```

require

Compliance

4 5 NT

Syntax

Category `named unary operator (module)`
Arguments `expression`
Arguments `none`
Return Value `1 (true) '' (false)`

Definition

If the expression is a scalar, the library specified by the `filename` is included (if it has not already been).

In Perl 5, if the expression is numeric this requires that the version of Perl being used (in `$PERL_VERSION` or `$[`) is greater than or equal to the version specified.

Note that Perl 5 also has the `use()` mechanism for including modules; `use()` is more robust than `require`.

Example

```
require "cgilib.pl";
```

reset

Compliance

4 5 NT

Syntax

Category `named unary operator (misc)`
Arguments `expression`
Arguments `none`
Return Value `1`

Definition

This function provides a way of resetting variables in the current package (especially pattern match variables). The expression is interpreted as a list of single characters. All variables starting with those characters are reset. The letters are case sensitive (as Perl variables are). Hyphens may be used to specify ranges of variables to reset. If called without any argument, `reset` simply resets all search matches.

CAUTION Use of this operator can reset system variables you may not want to alter. For example, be very careful with the following:

```
reset A-Z;
```

return

Compliance

4 5 NT

Syntax

Category `list operator (flow)`
Arguments `list`
Return Value `list`

Definition

This function returns from a subroutine (or an `eval()`) with the value specified.

Example

```
sub test {
   return 1;
}
$test = &test;
print("return() Returned $test \n");
```

reverse

Compliance

4 5 NT

Syntax

Category `list operator (list)`
Arguments `list`
Return Value `list`

Definition

The `reverse` function returns the list given as an argument in reverse order. In a scalar context, it reverses the letters of its first argument.

Example

```
@a = (1,2,3);
print("reverse() ",reverse(@a),"\n");
```

rewinddir

Compliance

4 5 NT

Syntax

Category `named unary operator (i/o)`
Arguments `dirhandle`
Return Value `1 (true) '' (false)`

Definition

When reading a directory using `readdir()`, it is possible to reset the directory to the first file name.

Example

```
opendir(DIR,"/tmp");
print("rewinddir() (a): "
file: while ($file=readdir(DIR) {
   print $file, " ";
}
rewinddir();
print(" (b): "
file: while ($file=readdir(DIR) {
   print $file, " ";
}
print("\n");
closedir(DIR);
```

rindex

Compliance

[4] 5 NT

Syntax

Category `list operator (string)`
Arguments `string, substring, position`
Arguments `string, substring`
Return Value `position`

Definition

This function is very similar to `index()` except that, instead of scanning for the `substring` from the first character in the string, it scans backwards from the last character. So it returns the starting position of the last occurrence of `substring` in `string` (scanning backwards from the specified position or from the end if no position is specified).

Example

```
$ans1 = rindex("abcdefghijiklmdef:-)","def");
$ans2 = rindex("abcdefghijiklmdef","def",$ans1+3);
```

```
print("rindex() def is at $ans1 and next at
$ans2\n");
```

rmdir

Compliance

4 5 NT

Syntax

Category named unary operator (files)
Arguments filename
Return Value 1 or 0

Definition

This function deletes the directory specified (or `$_`) if it is empty and sets `$OS_ERROR` (`$!`) to the error value if there is a system error.

s///

Compliance

4 5 NT

Syntax

Category (pattern)
Arguments s/pattern/replacement/options
Return Value numeric

Definition

This function searches the default string for `pattern` (a regular expression) and replaces this with the `replacement` string (the actual replacemnt behavior depends on the `options`). It returns the number of replacements made. The default string is set using either of the pattern binding operators (=~ or ¬~) or `$_` is used if none have been bound. The valid options are

Option	Description
e	Evaluate the right side as an expression
g	Global (replace all occurrences)
i	Case-insensitive pattern matching
m	Ignore \n in string (multiple lines)
o	Optimize (compile pattern once)
s	Treat string as single line
x	Extended regular expressions

Example

```
$oldstr = "abcdefABCDEFabcdefABCDEF";
$newstr= $oldstr;
$str =~ s/abc/zzz/ig;
print("s/// $oldstr became $newstr \n");
```

scalar

Compliance

[4] 5 NT

Syntax

Category `named unary operator (misc)`
Arguments `expression`
Return Value `value`

Definition

This operator forces the argument to be interpreted in a scalar context, rather than as a list so that it can override the default context if necessary.

seek

Compliance

[4] 5 NT

Syntax

Category `list operator (i/o)`
Arguments `handle, position, start`
Return Value `1 (true) '' (false)`

Definition

This function sets the file pointer to a specified offset `position` in a file. The offset is relative to the `start` that can have three values: `0` (start of file), `1` (current position), `2` (end of file). This allows the use of random access files, and the implementation of fast read algorithms (for example binary search techniques) on file `handles`, especially with fixed-length data where the offsets are easier to calculate.

seekdir

Compliance

[4] 5 NT

Syntax

Category `list operator (i/o)`
Arguments `dirhandle, position`
Return Value `1 (true) '' (false)`

Definition

This function allows the position in a directory to be reset to a position saved with `telldir()`. This is useful when processing directories with `readdir()`.

select

Compliance

[4] 5 NT

Syntax

Category `named unary operator (i/o)`
Arguments `handle`
Arguments `rbits, wbits, ebits, timeout`
Return Value `handle`

Definition

This operator selects the default file `handle` used for I/O operations such as `print()` and `write()`. By default `STDOUT` is selected, but this function can select any other file handle to be the default instead. The return value is the currently selected file `handle` (before any change) so it is useful to assign this to a variable in order to be able to restore the original `handle` as the default at a later stage.

The second form calls the UNIX system `select()` function.

Example

```
open(OUT,"/tmp/t.out");
$return = select(OUT);
print("This goues in /tmp/t.out.\n");
select($return);
print("select() restored to STDOUT.\n");
```

semctl

Compliance

[4] 5

Syntax

Category `list operator (System V)`
Arguments `id, semnum, command, arg`
Return Value `value`

Definition

This function is equivalent to the UNIX `semctl()` function. This is a semaphore control operation with several variables.

semget

Compliance

[4] 5

Syntax

Category `list operator (System V)`
Arguments `key, nsems, flags`
Return Value `value`

Definition

This function is equivalent to the UNIX `semget()` function and returns the semaphore ID.

semop

Compliance

[4] 5

Syntax

Category list operator (System V)
Arguments key, opstring
Return Value 1 (true) '' (false)

Definition

The semop function is equivalent to the UNIX semop() function call and performs semaphore signalling and waiting functions.

send

Compliance

[4] 5

Syntax

Category list operator (socket)
Arguments socket, message, flags, to
Arguments socket, message, flags
Return Value numeric

Definition

This function is equivalent to the UNIX system send() function and sends a message socket.

setgrent

Compliance

4 5

Syntax

Category `(system files)`
Arguments `none`
Return Value `n/a`

Definition

This function rewinds the `/etc/group` file to the start of the file for subsequent accesses using `getgrent()`.

Example

```
print("setgrent() ",setgrent(), "\n");
```

sethostent

Compliance

[4] 5

Syntax

Category `named unary operator (system files)`
Arguments `flag`
Return Value `N/A`

Definition

If called with an argument of `1`, this function tells the system to keep a TCP socket open for name server queries such as `gethostbyname()`. If this is not, then the name server queries use UDP datagrams.

Example

```
print("sethostent() ",sethostent(1), "\n");
```

setnetent

Compliance

[4] 5

Syntax

Category `named unary operator (system files)`
Arguments `flag`
Return Value `N/A`

Definition

This function rewinds the `/etc/networks` file used by `getnetent()` and other network related functions. If the flag has a value of `1`, then the file is kept open between calls to `getnetbyname()` and `getnetbyaddr()`.

```
print("setnetent() ",setnetent(1), "\n");
```

setpgrp

Compliance

[4] 5

Syntax

Category `list operator (process)`
Arguments `pid, pgrp`
Return Value `1 (true) '' (false)`

Definition

This function sets the current process group for the specified process (`pid`); if this is zero, the current process is set.

setpriority

Compliance

[4] 5

Syntax

Category `list operator (proxess)`
Arguments `type, id, priority`
Return Value `1 (true) '' (false)`

Definition

This function calls the UNIX `setprority()` function. The `type` is one of `PRIO_PROCESS`, `PRIO_PGGRP`, or `PRIO_USER`. The `id` is the relevent ID for this (`pid`, a `pid` for a group of processes, or `uid`). If `0` is used as the `id`, the current process, process group, or user is used. The `priority` is a number representing the level of priority (normally in the range `120` to `20`) where the lower the priority, the more favorable the scheduling of the process by the operating system.

Example

```
print("setpriority() ",setpriority(0,0,-20),"\n");
```

setprotoent

Compliance

[4] 5

Syntax

Category `named unary operator (system files)`
Arguments `flag`
Return Value `1 (true) '' (false)`

Definition

This function rewinds the `/etc/protocols` file used by `getprotoent()` and other protocol related functions. If the `flag` has a value of `1`, then the file is kept open between calls to `getprotobyname()` and `getnetbynumber()`.

Example

```
print("setprotoent() ",setprotoent(1), "\n");
```

setpwent

Compliance

[4] 5

Syntax

Category `(system files)`
Arguments `none`
Return Value `1 (true) '' (false)`

Definition

This function rewinds the `/etc/passwd` file used by `getpwent()` and other password related functions.

Example

```
print("setpwent() ",setpwent(), "\n");
```

setservent

Compliance

[4] 5

Syntax

Category named unary operator (system files)
Arguments flag
Return Value 1 (true) '' (false)

Definition

This function rewinds the /etc/services file used by getservent() and other service-related functions. If the flag has a value of 1, then the file is kept open between calls to getservbyname() and getnetbyport().

Example

```
print("setservent() ",setservent(1), "\n");
```

setsockopt

Compliance

[4] 5

Syntax

Category list operator (socket)
Arguments socket, level, optname, optval
Return Value 1 (true) '' (false)

Definition

This function is equivalent to UNIX system call `setsockopt()` and sets the socket options.

shift

Compliance

4 5 NT

Syntax

Category `named unary operator (array)`
Arguments `array`
Arguments `none`
Return Value `value`

Definition

This function takes the leftmost element from the `array` specified and returns that, reducing the array by one element. When no `array` is specified, the array of arguments passed to the Perl script, `$ARGV`, is used if the context is not in a subroutine; otherwise, the array of arguments passed to the subroutine, `@_`, is used.

The return value is undefined if the array is empty.

Example

```
print("shift() ");
while ($arg = shift) {
   print($arg,' ');
}
print("\n");
```

shmctl

Compliance

[4] 5

Syntax

Category `list operator (System V)`
Arguments `id, cmd, arg`
Return Value `value`

Definition

This function is equivalent to the UNIX `shmctl()` function and performs shared memory control operations.

shmget

Compliance

[4] 5

Syntax

Category `list operator (System V)`
Arguments `key.size, flags`
Return Value `value`

Definition

This function is equivalent to the UNIX `shmget()` function and returns shared memory segment ID.

shmread

Compliance

[4] 5

Syntax

Category `list operator (System V)`
Arguments `id, var. pos, size`
Return Value `value`

Definition

This function is equivalent to the UNIX `shmread()` function and reads from the shared memory segment ID.

shmwrite

Compliance

[4] 5

Syntax

Category `list operator (System V)`
Arguments `id, string, pos, size`
Return Value `value`

Definition

This function is equivalent to the UNIX `shmwrite()` function and writes to the shared memory segment ID.

shutdown

Compliance

[4] 5 NT

Syntax

Category `list operator (socket)`
Arguments `socket, how`
Return Value `1 (true) '' (false)`

Definition

This function is equivalent to the UNIX `shutdown()` function and shuts down a socket.

sin

Compliance

4 5 NT

Syntax

Category `named unary operator (numeric)`
Arguments `expression`
Arguments `none`
Return Value `numeric`

Definition

This function returns the sine of the expression in radians. If there is no explicit argument, `$_` is used.

Example

```
print("sin() ",sin(4), "\n");
```

sleep

Compliance

4 5 NT

Syntax

Category `named unary operator (process)`
Arguments `expression`
Arguments `none`
Return Value `numeric`

Definition

This function causes the current process to `sleep` for the number of seconds specified in `expression` (if none is specified, it sleeps forever but may be woken up by a signal if this has been programmed).

Example

```
print("sleep() ",sleep(5),"\n");
```

socket

Compliance

[4] 5 NT

Syntax

Category `list operator (socket)`
Arguments `socket, domain, type, protocol`
Return Value `value`

Definition

This function is equivalent to the UNIX `socket()` system call and opens a specified type of socket and attaches it to a file handle.

socketpair

Compliance

[4] 5

Syntax

Category `list operator (socket)`
Arguments `socket1, socket2, domain, type, protocol`
Return Value `value`

Definition

This function is equivalent to the UNIX `socketpair()` system call and creates a pair of sockets, which are unnamed, in the specified `domain`.

sort

Compliance

4 5 NT

Syntax

Category `list operator (list)`
Arguments `subname list`
Arguments `block list`
Arguments `list`
Return Value `list`

Definition

This function sorts the list specified and returns the sorted list. The sort method can be specified with the optional subroutine or block argument. A subroutine may be specified that takes two arguments (passed as global package variables, `$a $b`) and returns `TRUE` if the first is less than or equal to the second by any criteria used. Similarly, a block can be specified (effectively an anonymous subroutine) to perform this function. The default sort order is based on the standard string comparison order.

Example

```
@a = ("z","w","r","i","b","a");
print("sort() ",sort(@a),"\n");
```

splice

Compliance

[4] 5 NT

Syntax

Category `list operator (array)`
Arguments `array, offset, length, list`
Arguments `array, offset, length`
Arguments `array, offset`
Return Value `list`

Definition

This function removes the elements specified by `offset` and `length` from the array and replaces them with the elements in the list supplied as the last argument. A list of those elements removed is returned. If no `length` is specified, all the items from `offset` to the end of the array are removed.

Example

```
@a = ("a","e","i","o","u");
print("splice() ",splice(@a,0,3,"A","E","I"),"\n");
```

split

Compliance

4 5 NT

Syntax

Category list operator (pattern)
Arguments /pattern/,expression,limit
Arguments /pattern/,expression
Arguments /pattern/
Arguments none
Return Value list

Definition

This function manipulates a string, splitting the string denoted by the expression (or the $_ if none is specified) into an array of strings based on some separator string specified by the pattern (if the pattern has no specified whitespace as the default). An optional limit restricts the number of elements returned. A negative limit has no effect.

If not in a list context, the number of elements found is returned. In an scalar context, it returns the number of elements and puts the resulting array into the @_ array (the use of the @_ as the result is depreciated).

Examples

```
print("spilt() ",split(/:/,"1:2:3:4:5"),"\n");
```

sprintf

Compliance

[4] 5 NT

Syntax

Category `list operator (string)`
Arguments `format, list`
Return Value `string`

Definition

This is equivalent to the C `sprintf()` call. The format is a string with special metacharacters to specify how may values/variables follow and how to represent each of these in the resulting string. This enables the explicit formatting of floating point and integer numbers (also enabling binary, hexidecimal, and octal formats).

Example

```
print("strintf() ",sprintf("%0d \n",9),"\n");
```

sqrt

Compliance

4 5 NT

Syntax

Category `named unary operator (numeric)`
Arguments `expression`
Return Value `numeric`

Definition

This function returns the result of evaluating the expression and finding its square root.

Example

```
print("sqrt() ",sqrt(4),"\n");
```

srand

Compliance

4 5 NT

Syntax

Category `named unary operator (numeric)`
Arguments `expression`
Arguments `none`
Return Value `1 (true) '' (false)`

Definition

This function sets the seed used by the pseudorandom number generation algorithm when generating `rand()` numbers. In order to randomize the possible sequences, the seed should be set to a different value each time the script is called. The default behavior, when no expression is supplied, is to use the result of a call to `time()`. This is not a secure method of randomizing for scripts that need to be secure because it is possible to predict what sequence the script will return.

Note that, when using a set of pseudorandom data generated using `rand()`, it is possible to generate exactly the same data repeatedly (without having to save the entire sequence) simply by stetting and saving the seed. Restoring the seed and calling `rand()` will then produce the same sequence again.

Example

```
srand(26);
print("rand() ",rand(),", ");
srand(26);
print(rand()," (should produce the same \"random\"
number twice) \n");
```

stat

Compliance

4 5 NT

Syntax

Category `list operator (files)`
Arguments `handle`
Arguments `expression`
Arguments `none`
Return Value `list`

Definition

This function returns the file statistics of the file pointed to by the file `handle` (or a file `handle` produced by evaluating the expression). Note that, like the file test operators, `stat()` can take a special argument underscore; this means that the test is carried out on the same file `handle` as the last `file test`, `stat()`, or `lstat()` call.

Example

```
($device,$inode,$mode,$nlink,$uid,$gid,$rdev,$size,$atime,
    $mtime,$ctime,$blksize,$blocks) = stat("/etc/
    passwd");
print("stat() $device, $inode, $ctime \n");
```

study

Compliance

4 5 NT

Syntax

Category `named unary operator (pattern)`
Arguments `scalar`
Arguments `none`
Return Value `1 (true) '' (false)`

Definition

When many pattern match operations are being performed on the same string, the efficiency of these patterns can be improved with the `study()` function. If no string is specified, the `$_` is studied by default. The call sets up internal lookup tables based on the string studied so that pattern matching operations can use this information to process the pattern match more quickly. Only one string at a time can be studied (subsequent calls effectively "unstudy" any previous `study()` removing the lookup tables). The function `study()` is often used in a loop processing lines of a text file where each line is studied before being processed with various pattern matches.

sub

Compliance

4 5 NT

Syntax

Category `(flow)`
Arguments `name block`

Arguments `name`
Arguments `name`
Return Value `value`

Definition

This is the syntax for a subroutine declaration. The full form defines a subroutine with the `name` and associates this with the statements in block. When evoked, it will return the result of the last statement executed in the block (often a `return()` statement). If no name is supplied, it is an anonymous subroutine (certain functions such as `sort()` allow anonymous subroutines as arguments). With only a name as an argument, the statement is a forward reference to a subroutine, which is fully declared later in the script.

substr

Compliance

[4] 5 NT

Syntax

Category `list operator (string)`
Arguments `expression, offset, length`
Arguments `expression, offset`
Return Value `string`

Definition

This function returns a substring of a string specified by expression. The substring starts at the specified `offset` and has the specified `length`. If the offset is negative, it starts from the right side of the string instead of the left side. If the length is negative, it means to trim the string by that number of characters.

Example

```
print("substr() ",substring("okay",0,2),"\n");
```

symlink

Compliance

[4] 5

Syntax

Category `list operator ((files)`
Arguments `oldfile, newfile`
Return Value `1 or 0`

Definition

This function creates a symbolic link from the existing file specified by `oldfile` to the specified `newfile` and returns `1` on success and `0` on failure. If symbolic links are not supported by the operating system, this will return a fatal error.

Example

```
print("symlink() ",symlink("/usr/local","/tmp/
symlinktousrlocal"),"\n");
```

syscall

Compliance

4 5

Syntax

Category `list operator (i/o)`
Arguments `list`
Return Value `varies`

Definition

This mechanism allows Perl to call corresponding UNIX C system calls directly. It relies on the existence of the set of Perl header files Syscall.ph which declares all of these calls. The script `h2ph` that is normally executed when Perl is installed, sets up the Syscall.ph files. Each call has the same name as the equivalent UNIX system call with the `SYS_` prefix. As these calls actually pass control to the relevant C system function. Care must be taken with passing parameters.

The fisrt element in the list used as an argument to `syscall()` itself, is the name corresponding to the UNIX system call (that is, with the `SYS_` prefix). The next elements in the list are interpreted as parameters to this call. Numeric values are passed as the C type `int`. String values are passed as pointers to arrays. The length of these strings must be able to cope with any value assigned to that parameter in the call.

Example

```
require "syscall.ph";
print("syscall() ",syscall(&SYS_getpid)," equiva-
lent to $PID\n");
```

sysopen

Compliance

[4] 5

Syntax

Category `list operator (i/o)`
Arguments `handle, name, mode, permissions`
Arguments `handle, name, mode`
Return Value `1 (true) '' (false)`

Definition

This function calls the UNIX C `open()` function directly from the Perl script, which opens a file for reading or writing.

sysread

Compliance

[4] 5

Syntax

Category `list operator (i/o)`
Arguments `handle, scalar, length, offset`
Arguments `handle, scalar, length`
Return Value `1 (true) '' (false)`

Definition

This function calls the UNIX C `read()` function directly from the Perl script, which reads a line from the standard input source.

system

Compliance

4 5 NT

Syntax

Category `list operator (process)`
Arguments `list`
Return Value `status`

Definition

This call executes the specified list as an operating system call. The process to execute this command is forked and the script waits for the child process to return. The return value is the exit status of the child process.

NOTE To capture the output from a system call, use the `qx//` (back quote mechanism) rather than `system()`.

Example

```
print("system() ",system("ls -F /var > /tmp/
t.tmp"),"\n");
```

syswrite

Compliance

[4] 5

Syntax

Category `list operator (i/o)`
Arguments `handle, scalar, length, offset`
Arguments `handle, scalar, length`
Return Value `1 (true) '' (false)`

Definition

This function calls the UNIX C `write()` function directly from the Perl script, which is an interactive write to another user process.

tell

Compliance

4 5 NT

Syntax

Category `named unary operator (i/o)`
Arguments `expression`

Arguments none
Return Value position

Definition

This function returns the current position in the file specified by the expression (which should evaluate to a file `handle`). If no `handle` is specified, the last file accessed is used. This value can be used by `seek()` to return to this position if appropriate.

Example

```
print("tell() ",tell(STDOUT),"\n");
```

telldir

Compliance

4 5 NT

Syntax

Category named unary operator (i/o)
Arguments dirhandle
Return Value position

Definition

This function returns the current position in the directory `handle` specified. This value can be used by `seekdir()` to return to this position if appropriate.

Example

```
opendir(DIR,"/tmp");
readdir(DIR);
print("telldir() ",telldir(DIR),"\n");
```

tie

Compliance

5 NT

Syntax

Category `list operator (class)`
Arguments `variable, classname, list`
Return Value `object`

Definition

This function binds a variable to a package class. It creates an instance of this class by running the `new()` method associated with that class. Any parameters for the `new()` method may be specified in the list.

The behavior depends on the way the package class is written and on the type of variable. Most common are package classes written to support associative arrays. In particular, package classes exist to bind associative arrays to various databases.

The `tie()` mechanism hides all the complexities of implemention behind a simple interface so that, for example, the records in a database can be accessed by looking at the associative array bound to the database though an appropriate package class.

The example here uses the Configure.pm module. This module gives access to information about the machine on which Perl was installed. It is possible to bind an associative array to this class and examine this to find out the value of any of the configuration parameters.

Example

```
use Configure;
$return = tie %c, Configure;
print("tie() returned \"$return\" and ",
    "a sample value is $c{installbin}\n");
```

tied

Compliance

5 NT

Syntax

Category `named unary operator`
Arguments `variable`
Return Value `object`

Definition

This function was first implemented in Perl 5.002 and returns a reference to the object that the variable is an instance of. This is the same as is returned by the original call to `tie()` when it is bound.

time

Compliance

4 5 NT

Syntax

Category `(time)`
Arguments `none`
Return Value `time`

Definition

This function returns the time, in seconds, since 1 January 1970. The format can be converted into more useful parts using `gmtime()` or `localtime()`.

times

Compliance

4 5

Syntax

Category (process)
Arguments none
Return Value list

Definition

This function returns a list of four elements representing the time, in seconds, used. The four elements represent the system time and the user time used by the current process and child processes.

Example

```
($usertime,$systemtime,$childsystem,$childuser) =
times();
print("times() $usertime $systemtime $childsystem
$childuser\n");
```

tr///

Compliance

4 5 NT

Syntax

Category (string)
Arguments tr/searchlist/replacelist/<options>
Return Value numeric

Definition

This function translates all occurrences of items in the search list with the equivalent items in the replacement list. The string searched is the default search string bound by =~ or !=, or if no string is bound to the pattern match, the $_ string is used. The return value is the number of characters translated or deleted.

The valid options are

Option	Description
c	Complement (non-matching characters in search list are used)
d	Delete (delete any characters not in search list as well as translating)
s	Squash (if the translation results in a sequence of repeated characters from the replace list ,then reduce this to one occurance of the character)

The `searchlist` and the `replacelist` may contain the character to indicate a range of characters.

Examples

```
tr/AEIOU/aeiou/  # Make all vowels lowercase
tr/[A-M]/[a-m]/  # Make first half of alphabet
                 lowercase
tr/aeiou/ /c     # Replace all non-vowels with
                                      space
tr/aeiou/AEIOU/d # Make all vowels uppercase and
                 # remove all other characters
tr/aeiou/-/s     # Replace all vowels with -,
                 # but only one - for adjacent
                 vowels
```

truncate

Compliance

[4] 5 NT

Syntax

Category `list operator (i/o)`
Arguments `handle, length`
Arguments `expression, length`
Return Value `1 (true) '' (false)`

Definition

This function truncates the file referenced by the file `handle` to `length`. An expression can be used that evaluates to the file `handle` if the operating system does not implement this feature.

uc

Compliance

5 NT

Syntax

Category `named unary operator (string)`
Arguments `expression`
Return Value `string`

Definition

This function returns an uppercase version of the specified `expression`.

Example

```
print("uc() ",uc("This is All Caps"), "\n");
```

ucfirst

Compliance

5 NT

Syntax

Category `named unary operator (string)`
Arguments `expression`
Return Value `string`

Definition

This function returns a `string` with the first character of the `expression` in uppercase.

Example

```
print("ucfirst() ",ucfirst("this is Capitalized"),
"\n");
```

umask

Compliance

4 5

Syntax

Category `named unary operator (files)`
Arguments `newumask`
Arguments `none`
Return Value `oldumask`

Definition

This function sets the file mask using the specified `newumask`. It returns the `oldumask` so that it can be stored and restored later if required. If called without any arguments, it returns the current umask. This is the mechanism UNIX uses to modify the permissions of any files created.

Example

```
print("umask() The current umask is: ",umask,"\n");
```

undef

Compliance

4 5 NT

Syntax

Category `named unary operator (misc)`
Arguments `expression`
Arguments `none`
Return Value `value`

Definition

This function undefines the value of the expression. The expression may be a scalar value, and array, or a subroutine (specified with an & prefix). When called without an expression, this function returns an undefined value.

unlink

Compliance

4 5 NT

Syntax

Category `list operator (files)`
Arguments `list`
Return Value `numeric`

Definition

This function deletes the files in the `list` and returns the number of files deleted.

Example

```
system("touch /tmp/t.tst");
print("unlink() ",unlink("/tmp/t.tst"),"\n");
```

unpack

Compliance

[4] 5 NT

Syntax

Category `list operator (data)`
Arguments `template, expression`
Return Value `list`

Definition

This function unpacks data that are packed with `pack()`. It uses the same template mechanism to specify the format of the data in the packed string. In a scalar context, the first value in the list is returned.

unshift

Compliance

[4] 5 NT

Syntax

Category list operator (array)
Arguments array, list
Return Value numeric

Definition

This function prepends the list to the front of the specified `array` and returns the new number of elements in `array`.

Example

```
@a = (a, b, c);
$ret = unshift(@a, 1, 2, 3);
print("unshift() Array has $ret
elements:",@a,"\n");
```

untie

Compliance

5 NT

Syntax

Category named unary operator (class)
Arguments variable
Return Value 1 (true) '' (false)

Definition

This function undoes the binding between a variable and a `package` class that was created using `tie()`.

use

Compliance

5 NT

Syntax

Category `list operator (module)`
Arguments `module, list`
Return Value `N/A`

Definition

This function imports the specified module into the current block. The `import()` method defined for the package class represented by the module is evaluated. The specified list is passed as optional arguments to this `import()` method. If you do not specify a list argument, then the default methods for that module will be those imported. You can specify the empty `list()` in order to avoid adding any items to the local namespace.

Example

```
use English;
```

Note that this is the mechanism for implementing compiler directives known as pragmas. You can, for example, force all aritmateic to be interger based by

```
use integer;
```

And then this can be turned off again with

```
no integer;
```

utime

Compliance

4 5

Syntax

Category `list operator (files)`
Arguments `list`
Return Value `numeric`

Definition

This function sets the access and modification time of all the files in the `list` to the time specified in the first two items in the list. The time must be in the numeric format (that is, seconds since 1 January 1970) as returned by the `time()` function.

Example

```
$time = now;
print("utime() ",utime($time,$time,"/tmp/
t.tst"),"\n");
```

values

Compliance

4 5 NT

Syntax

Category `named unary operator (hash)`
Arguments `variable`
Return Value `list`

Definition

This function returns the array comprising all the values in the associate array specified. In a scalar context, it returns the number of values in the array.

Example

```
%a = (1, "one", 2, "two", 3, "three");
print("values() ",values(%a),"\n);
```

vec

Compliance

[4] 5 NT

Syntax

Category `list operator (fixed)`
Arguments `expression, offset, bits`
Return Value `value`

Definition

This function uses the string specified by `expression` as a vector of unsigned integers. The return value is the value of the bitfield specified by `offset`. The specified bits is the number of bits that are reserved for each entry in the bit vector. This must be a power of 2 from 1 to 32. Note that the `offset` is the marker for the end of the vector, and it counts back the number of bits specified to find the start.

Vectors can be manipulated with the logical bitwise operators |, &, and ^.

Example

```
$vec = '';
vec($vec,3,4) = 1;       # bits 0 to 3
vec($vec,7,4) = 10;      # bits 4 to 7
```

```
vec($vec,11,4) = 3;     # bits 8 to 11
vec($vec,15,4) = 15;    # bits 12 to 15
# As there are 4 bits per number this can be
decoded by
# unpack() as a hex number
print("vec() Has a created a string of nybbles, in
hex: ",
   unpack("h*",$vec),"\n");
```

wait

Compliance

4 5

Syntax

Category (process)
Arguments none
Return Value pid

Definition

This function waits for a child process to exit. It returns the process ID (`pid`) of the terminated process and `-1` if there are no child processes.

waitpid

Compliance

[4] 5

Syntax

Category `list operator (process)`
Arguments `pid, flags`
Return Value `pid`

Definition

This function waits for a specified child process to exit and returns `pid` of the terminated process and `-1` if there is no child process matching the `pid` specified. The flags can be set to various values that are equivalent to the `waitpid()` UNIX system call (if the operating system supports this), a flags value of 0 should work on all operating systems supporting processes.

wantarray

Compliance

4 **5** **NT**

Syntax

Category `(flow)`
Arguments `none`
Return Value `1 (true) '' (false)`

Definition

This function returns `1` if the current context is an array context; otherwise, it returns `''`. This construct is most often used to return two alternatives from a subroutine, depending on the calling context.

Example

```
return wantarray ? (8, 4, 33) : 3;
```

warn

Compliance

4 5 NT

Syntax

Category list operator (i/o)
Arguments list
Return Value 1 (true) '' (false)

Definition

This function prints the supplied list to STDERR, like die(). If there is no newline in the list, warn() appends the text at line <line number>\n to the message. However, the script will continue after a warn().

write

Compliance

4 5 NT

Syntax

Category list operator (i/o)
Arguments expression
Arguments handle
Arguments none

Definition

This function writes a formatted record to the file `handle` (or the file `handle` that the expression evaluates to). If no file `handle` is specified, the default is `STDOUT`; this can be altered using `select()` if necessary.

A format for use by that file `handle` must have been declared using the `format()` function. This defaults to the name of the file `handle` being used, but other format names can be associated with the current `write()` operation using the `$FORMAT_NAME` (`$~`) special variable.

y///

Compliance

4 **5** **NT**

Syntax

Category `(string)`
Arguments `y/searchlist/replacelist/<options>`
Return Value `numeric`

Definition

The `y///` operator is a synonym for the translation operator `tr///`.

Regular Expressions

A regular expression is a way of specifying a pattern so that some strings match the pattern and some strings do not. Parts of the matching pattern can be marked for use in operations such as substitution. This is a powerful tool for processing text, especially when producing text-based reports. Many UNIX utilities use a form of regular expressions as a pattern matching mechanism (for example, `egrep`) and Perl has adopted this concept, almost as its own.

Like arithmetic expressions, regular expressions are made up of a sequence of legal symbols linked with legal operators. This table lists all of these operators and symbols in one table for easy reference. If you are new to regular expressions you may find the description in "Perl Overview" informative.

Table 11 lists Perl's Regular Expressions.

Table 11 Regular Expression Meta-Characters, Meta-Brackets, and Meta-Sequences

Meta-Character	Description
^	This meta-character—the caret—will match the beginning of a string or, if the `/m` option is used, match the beginning of a line. It is one of two pattern anchors—the other anchor is the `$`.
.	This meta-character will match any single character except for the newline unless the `/s` option is specified. If the `/s` option is specified, then the newline will also be matched.
$	This meta-character will match the end of a string or, if the `/m` option is used, match the end of a line. It is one of two pattern anchors—the other anchor is the `^`.

continues

Table 12 Continued

Meta-Character	Description
|	This meta-character—called `alternation`_lets you specify two values that can cause the match to succeed. For instance, `m/a|b/` means that the `$_` variable must contain the "a" or "b" character for the match to succeed.
*	This meta-character indicates that the "thing" immediately to the left should be matched 0 or more times in order to be evaluated as true; thus, `.*` matches any number of character).
+	This meta-character indicates that the "thing" immediately to the left should be matched 1 or more times in order to be evaluated as true.
?	This meta-character indicates that the thing immediately to the left should be matched 0 or 1 times in order to be evaluated as true. When used in conjunction with the `+, ?, or {n, m}` meta-characters and brackets, it means that the regular expression should be non-greedy and match the smallest possible string.

Meta-Brackets	Description
()	The parentheses let you affect the order of pattern evaluation and act as a form of pattern memory. See the "Special Variables" chapter for more details.
(?...)	If a question mark immediately follows the left parentheses it indicates that an extended mode component is being specified (new to Perl 5).
(?#*comment*)	Extension: *comment* is any text.
(?:*regx*)	Extension: *regx* is any regular expression, but parentheses are not saved as a backreference.
(?=*regx*)	Extension: allows matching of zero-width positive lookahead characters (that is, the regular expression is matched but not returned as being matched).
(?!*regx*)	Extension: allows matching of zero-width negative lookahead characters (that is, negated form of `(=regx)`).

Meta-Brackets	Description
(?*options*)	Extension: applies the specified options to the pattern bypassing the need for the option to specified in the normal way. Valid *options* are: `i` (case insenstive), `m` (treat as multiple lines), `s` (treat as single line), `x` (allow whitespace and comments).
{n, m}	The braces let you specify how many times the "thing" immediately to the left should be matched. {*n*} means that it should be matched exactly n times. {*n*,} means it must be matched at least n times. {*n*, *m*} means that it must be matched at least *n* times but not more than *m* times.
[]	The square brackets let you create a character class. For instance, m/[abc]/ will evaluate to true if any of "a", "b", or "c" is contained in $_. The square brackets are a more readable alternative to the alternation meta-character.

Meta-Sequences	Description
\	This meta-character "escapes" the character that follows. This means that any special meaning normally attached to that character is ignored. For instance, if you need to include a dollar sign in a pattern, you must use `\$` to avoid Perl's variable interpolation. Use `\\` to specify the backslash character in your pattern.
\nnn	Any octal byte (where *nnn* represents the octal number—this allows any charcter to be specified by its octal number).
\a	The alarm character (this is a special character that, when printed, produces a warning bell sound).
\A	This meta-sequence represents the beginning of the string. Its meaning is not affected by the `/m` option.
\b	This meta-sequence represents the backspace character inside a character class, otherwise it represents a word boundary. A word boundary is the spot between word (`\w`) and non-word (`\W`)

continues

Table 12 Continued

Meta-Sequences	Description
	characters. Perl thinks that the W meta-sequence matches the imaginary characters of the end of the string.
\B	Match a non-word boundary.
\cn	Any control character (where *n* is the character, for example, `\cY` for Ctrl+Y).
\d	Match a single digit character.
\D	Match a single non-digit character.
\e	The escape character.
\E	Terminate the \L or \U sequence.
\f	The form feed character.
\G	Match only where the previous m //g left off.
\l	Change the next character to lower case.
\L	Change the following characters to lowercase until a \E sequence is encountered.
\n	The newline character.
\Q	Quote Regular Expression Meta-characters literally until the \E sequence is encountered.
\r	The carriage return character.
\s	Match a single whitespace character.
\S	Match a single non-whitespace character.
\t	The tab character.
\u	Change the next character to uppercase.
\U	Change the following characters to uppercase until a \E sequence is encountered.
\v	The vertical tab character.
\w	Match a single word character. Word characters are the alphanumeric and underscore characters.
\W	Match a single non-word character.

Meta-Sequences	Description
\xnn	Any hexadecimal byte.
\Z	This meta-sequence represents the end of the string. Its meaning is not affected by the /m option.
\$	The dollar character.
\@	The ampersand character.
\%	The percentcharacter.

REFERENCE TABLES

This chapter includes tables for two important areas of Perl programming. First, although regular expressions are explained in the "Perl Overview" chapter, it is useful to have a quick reference table for the various symbols and their meanings in regular expressions. Secondly, a list of the Perl 5 standard modules is included.

Regular Expressions

A regular expression is a way of specifying a pattern so that some strings match the pattern and some strings do not. Parts of the matching pattern can be marked for use in operations such as substitution. This is a powerful tool for processing text, especially when producing text-based reports. Many UNIX utilities, such as `egrep`, use a form of regular expressions as a pattern-matching mechanism, and Perl has adopted this concept, almost as its own.

Like arithmetic expressions, regular expressions are made up of a sequence of legal symbols linked with legal operators. Table 12 lists all of these operators and symbols in one table for easy reference. If you are new to regular expressions you may find the description in the "Perl Overview" chapter informative.

Table 12 Regular Expression Meta-Characters, Meta-Brackets, and Meta-Sequences

Meta-Character	Description
^	This meta-character, the caret, matches the beginning of a string or, if the `/m` option is used, match the beginning of a line. It is one of two pattern anchors, the other anchor is the `$`.

continues

Table 12 Continued

<table>
<tr><th>Meta-Character</th><th>Description</th></tr>
<tr><td>.</td><td>This meta-character will match any single character except for the newline character unless the /s option is specified. If the /s option is specified, then the newline will also be matched.</td></tr>
<tr><td>$</td><td>This meta-character will match the end of a string or, if the /m option is used, match the end of a line. It is one of two pattern anchors; the other anchor is the ^.</td></tr>
<tr><td>|</td><td>This meta-character, called alternation, lets you specify two values that can cause the match to succeed. For instance, m/a|b/ means that the $_ variable must contain the "a" or "b" character for the match to succeed.</td></tr>
<tr><td>*</td><td>This meta-character indicates that the "thing" immediately to the left should be matched zero or more times in order to be evaluated as true (thus .* matches any number of characters).</td></tr>
<tr><td>+</td><td>This meta-character indicates that the "thing" immediately to the left should be matched one or more times in order to be evaluated as true.</td></tr>
<tr><td>?</td><td>This meta-character indicates that the "thing" immediately to the left should be matched zero or one times to be evaluated as true. When used in conjunction with the +, ?, or {n, m} meta-characters and brackets, it means that the regular expression should be non-greedy and match the smallest possible string.</td></tr>
</table>

Meta-Brackets	Description
()	The parentheses let you affect the order of pattern evaluation and act as a form of pattern memory. See the "Special Variables" chapter for more details.
(?...)	If a question mark immediately follows the left parentheses, it indicates that an extended mode component is being specified; this is new to Perl 5.

Meta-Brackets	Description
(?#*comment*)	Extension: `comment` is any text.
(?:*regx*)	Extension: `regx` is any regular expression but () are not saved as a backreference.
(?=*regx*)	Extension: Allows matching of zero-width positive lookahead characters (that is, the regular expression is matched but not returned as being matched).
(?!*regx*)	Extension: Allows matching of zero-width negative lookahead characters (that is, negated form of (=`regx`)).
(?*options*)	Extension: Applies the specified `options` to the pattern bypassing the need for the option to specified in the normal way. Valid options are: `i` (case insenstive), `m` (treat as multiple lines), `s` (treat as single line), and `x` (allow whitespace and comments).
{n, m}	Braces let you specify how many times the "thing" immediately to the left should be matched. {`n`} means that it should be matched exactly `n` times. {`n`,} means it must be matched at least `n` times. {`n`, `m`} means that it must be matched at least `n` times but not more than `m` times.
[]	Square brackets let you create a character class. For instance, `m/[abc]/` evaluates to True if any of "a", "b", or "c" is contained in $_. The square brackets are a more readable alternative to the alternation meta-character.

Meta-Sequences	Description
\	This meta-character "escapes" the character which follows. This means that any special meaning normally attached to that character is ignored. For instance, if you need to include a dollar sign in a pattern, you must use \$ to avoid Perl's variable interpolation. Use \\ to specify the backslash character in your pattern.

continues

Table 12 Continued

Meta-Sequences	Description
nnn	Any octal byte where *nnn* represents the octal number; this allows any character to be specified by its octal number.
\a	The alarm character; this is a special character which, when printed, produces a warning bell sound.
\A	This meta-sequence represents the beginning of the string. Its meaning is not affected by the /m option.
\b	This meta-sequence represents the backspace character inside a character class; otherwise, it represents a word boundary. A word boundary is the spot between word (\w) and non-word (\W) characters. Perl thinks that the \W meta-sequence matches the imaginary characters of the end of the string.
\B	Match a non-word boundary.
\c*n*	Any control character where *n* is the character (for example, \cY for Ctrl+Y).
\d	Match a single digit character.
\D	Match a single non-digit character.
\e	The escape character.
\E	Terminate the \L or \U sequence.
\f	The form feed character.
\G	Match only where the previous m//g left off.
\l	Change the next character to lowercase.
\L	Change the following characters to lowercase until a \E sequence is encountered.
\n	The newline character.
\Q	Quote regular expression meta-characters literally until the \E sequence is encountered.
\r	The carriage return character.
\s	Match a single whitespace character.

Meta-Sequences	Description
\S	Match a single non-whitespace character.
\t	The tab character.
\u	Change the next character to uppercase.
\U	Change the following characters to uppercase until a `\E` sequence is encountered.
\v	The vertical tab character.
\w	Match a single word character. Word characters are the alphanumeric and underscore characters.
\W	Match a single non-word character.
\xnn	Any hexadecimal byte.
\Z	This meta-sequence represents the end of the string. Its meaning is not affected by the `/m` option.
\$	The dollar character.
\@	The ampersand character.
\%	The percent character.

Perl 5 Standard Modules

This is a list of the standard modules that come with Perl 5 along with a brief description.

For a list of all current modules, including many extra non-standard modules other than those listed here, see the CPAN archive. The contents of the Perl Module List at

ftp://ftp.funet.fi/pub/languages/perl/CPAN/modules/00modlist.long.html

The modules of the Perl Module List sorted by authors at

ftp://ftp.funet.fi/pub/languages/perl/CPAN/modules/by-authors

The modules of the Perl Module List sorted by category at

ftp://ftp.funet.fi/pub/languages/perl/CPAN/modules/by-category

The modules of the Perl Module List sorted by module at

ftp://ftp.funet.fi/pub/languages/perl/CPAN/modules/by-module

Module Name	Description
`AnyDBM_File`	Accesses external databases.
`AutoLoader`	Special way of loading subroutines on demand.
`AutoSplit`	Special way to set up modules for use of `AutoLoader`.
`Benchmark`	Time code for benchmarking.
`Carp`	Reports errors across modules.
`Config`	Reports compiler options used when Perl is installed.
`Cwd`	Functions to manipulate current directory.
`DB_File`	Accesses Berkley DB files.
`Devel::SelfStubber`	Allows correct inheritance autoloaded methods.
`diagnostics`	`pragma`; enables diagnostic warnings.
`DynaLoader`	Used by modules which link to C libraries.
`English`	`pragma`; allows the use of long special variable names.
`Env`	Allows access to environment variables.
`Exporter`	Standard way for modules to export subroutines.
`ExtUtils::Liblist`	Examines C libraries.
`ExtUtils::MakeMaker`	Creates Makefiles for extension modules.
`ExtUtils::Manifest`	Helps maintain a MANIFEST file.
`ExtUtils::Miniperl`	Used by Makefiles generated by `ExtUtils::MakeMaker`.
`ExtUtils::Mkbootstrap`	Used by Makefiles generated by `ExtUtils::MakeMaker`.
`Fcntl`	Accesses C's Fcntl.h.

Module Name	Description
`File::Basename`	Parses file names according to various operating system rules.
`File::CheckTree`	Multiple file tests.
`File::Find`	Finds files according to criteria.
`File::Path`	Creates/deletes directories.
`FileHandle`	Allows object syntax for file handles.
`Getopt::Long`	Uses `POSIX` style command-line options.
`Getopt::Std`	Uses single letter command-line options.
`I18N::Collate`	Uses `POSIX` local rules for sorting 8-bit strings.
`integer`	`pragma`; uses integer arithmetic.
`IPC::Open2`	Inter-Process Communications (process with read/write).
`IPC::Open3`	Inter-Process Communications (process with read/write/error).
`less`	`pragma`; unimplemented.
`Net::Ping`	Tests network node.
`overload`	Allows overloading of operators (that is, special behavior depending on object type).
`POSIX`	Uses `POSIX` standard identifiers.
`Safe`	Can evaluate Perl code in safe memory compartments.
`SelfLoader`	Allows specification of code to be autoloaded in module (alternative to the AutoLoader procedure).
`sigtrap`	`pragma`; initializes some signal handlers.

Module Name	Description
`Socket`	Accesses C's Socket.h.
`strict`	`pragma`; forces safe code.
`subs`	`pragma`, predeclares specified subroutine names.
`Test::Harness`	Runs the standard Perl tests.
`Text::Abbrev`	Creates an abbreviation table.

GLOSSARY

This glossary covers the terms used in describing the Perl language, and common terms used on the Internet that may be useful when locating and installing Perl or searching for Perl utilities or modules on the Network.

account A user ID and disk area restricted for the use of a particular person. Usually password protected.

alias A short name used to represent a more complicated one. Often used for mail addresses or host domain names.

alphanumeric character A character that is a single letter or a single digit.

analog A form of electronic communication using a continuous electromagnetic wave, such as television or radio. Any continuous wave form, as opposed to digital on/off transmissions.

archive A repository of files available for access at an Internet site. Also, a collection of files, often a backup of a disk or files saved to tape to allow them to be transferred.

argument A parameter passed to a subroutine or function.

ARPA (**Advanced Research Projects Agency**) a government agency that originally funded the research on the ARPANET (became DARPA in the mid-1970s).

ARPANET An experimental communications network funded by the government that eventually developed into the Internet.

array Data structure enumerating a number of elements indicated in Perl with an @ sign at the start of the variable name.

array context An array value is required (either a normal array or an associative array, both of which are lists).

article Message submitted to a UseNet newsgroup. Unlike an e-mail message that goes to a specific person or group of persons, a newsgroup message goes to directories (on many machines) that can be read by any number of people.

ASCII Data that is limited to letters, numbers, and punctuation.

attribute A form of a command-line switch as applied to tags in the HTML language. HTML commands or tags can be more specific when attributes are used. Not all HTML tags utilize attributes.

associative array Data structure enumerating a number of elements each associated with a key indicated in Perl with a % at the start of the variable name.

associativity A term to describe the way an operator takes its operands.

awk UNIX text processing utility program.

bang A slang term for an exclamation point.

bang address A type of e-mail address that separates host names in the address with exclamation points. Used for mail sent to the UUCP network, where specifying the exact path of the mail (including all hosts that pass on the message) is necessary. The address is in the form of machine!machine!userID, where the number of machines listed depends on the connections needed to reach the machine where the account userID is.

binary Data that may contain non-printable characters, including graphics files, programs, and sound files.

BinHex A program that is used to encode binary files as ASCII so that they can be sent through e-mail.

bit The basic unit of digital communications. There are 8 bits in a byte.

BITNET (Because It's Time Network) A non-TCP/IP network for small universities without Internet access.

bitwise functions Functions that treat their arguments as an array of binary bits.

bitwise operators Operators that treat their operands as an array of binary bits.

block A group of statements enclosed in braces.

bookmarks Term used by some World Wide Web browsers for marking URLs you access frequently.

Boolean logic Logic dealing with True/False values (for example, the operators AND, OR, and NOT are Boolean operators).

bounce An e-mail message you receive that tells you that an e-mail message you sent wasn't delivered. Usually contains an error code and the contents of the message that wasn't delivered.

bps (bits per second) A unit of measurement that expresses the speed at which data is transferred between computers.

bridge A device that connects one physical section of a network to another, often providing isolation.

browser A utility that lets you look through collections of things. For example, a file browser lets you look through a file system. Applications that let you access the World Wide Web are called browsers.

byte A digital storage unit large enough to contain one ASCII character. Compare to *bit*.

C A programming language that was the basis for many Perl features.

CERN The European Laboratory for Particle Physics, where the World Wide Web was first conceived of and implemented.

child A subprocess.

client User of a service. Also often refers to a piece of software that gets information from a server.

command line Line on a terminal-based interface where you enter commands to the operating system.

compress A program that compacts a file so it fits into a smaller space. Also can refer to the technique of reducing the amount of space a file takes up.

CompuServe A commercial online service that gives its subscribers access to the Internet in addition to its other features.

concatenate To join two strings.

context Many functions return either array values or scalar values depending on the context, that is, whether returning an array or a scalar value is appropriate for the place where the call was made.

CPAN (**Central Perl Archive Network**) a series of machines on the Internet that act as central repositories for Perl distributions, documentation, libraries, and modules. The master site is at **ftp://ftp.funet.fi/pub/languages/perl/CPAN/**, but many mirror sites exist in other countries.

cyberspace A term used to refer to the entire collection of sites accessible electronically. If your computer is attached to the Internet or another large network, it exists in cyberspace.

database An structured way of storing data in an organized way, often described in terms of a number of tables each made up of a series of records, each record being made of a number of fields.

data type Perl has three basic data types: scalar ($), array (@), and associative array (%), that is, these are the different kinds of variables that Perl can use.

daemon A program that runs automatically on a computer to perform a service for the operating system.

DARPA (Defense Advanced Research Projects Agency, originally ARPA) The government agency that funded the research that developed the ARPANET.

DBM A UNIX database format.

debugging The process of tracking down errors in a program, often aided by examining or outputting extra information designed to help this process.

dedicated line See *leased line*.

DES (Data Encryption Standard) An algorithm developed by the U.S. government to provide security for data transmitted over a network.

dialup A type of connection where you use a modem to connect to another computer or an Internet provider via phone lines.

digest A form of mailing list where a number of messages are concatenated (linked) and sent out as a single message.

digital Type of communications used by computers, consisting of individual on and off pulses. Compare to *analog*.

directory In most computer file systems files are grouped into a hierarchical tree structure with a number of files in each directory (the files are like the leaves and the directories are like the branches of this tree).

directory handle A link between a Perl program and a directory that is created when the directory is opened.

DNS See *Domain Name System (DNS)*.

DOD (Department of Defense) A U.S. government agency that originally sponsored the ARPANET research.

domain Highest subdivision of the Internet, for the most part by country (except in the U.S., where it's by type of organization, such as educational, commercial, and government). Usually the last part of a host name; for example, the domain part of **ibm.com** is .com, which represents the domain of commercial sites in the U.S.

Domain Name System (DNS) The system that translates between Internet IP address and Internet host names.

dot address See *host address*.

download Move a file from a remote computer to your local computer.

effective GID The group identifier of the current process, which may have been changed from the original GID by various means.

effective UID The user identifier of the current process, which may have been changed from the original UID by various means.

egrep A UNIX pattern matching utility that finds matching patterns in text files.

e-mail An electronic message delivered from one computer user to another. Short for electronic mail.

e-mail address An address used to send e-mail to a user on the Internet, consisting of the user name and host name (and any other necessary information, such as a gateway machine). An Internet e-mail address is usually of the form username@hostname.

emoticon See *smiley face*.

encryption The process of scrambling a message so that it can be read only by someone who knows how to unscramble it.

environment Every process has a number of variables associated with it, these are described as the environment; Perl provides ways of examining and changing these environment variables.

ethernet A type of local area network hardware. Many TCP/IP networks are ethernet based.

expire Remove an article from a UseNet newsgroup after a specified interval.

FAQ (Frequently Asked Question document, pronounced as fak) Contains a list of commonly asked questions on a topic. Most UseNet newsgroups have a FAQ to introduce new readers to popular topics in the newsgroup.

feed Send UseNet newsgroups from your site to another site that wants to read them.

FIFO (First-In First-Out) A queue where the first item placed in the queue is the first item processed when the queue is processed.

file Basic unit of storage of computer data in a file structure; files can normally be binary or text only (ASCII).

file handle A link between a Perl program and a file that is created when the file is opened.

file test Perl has a number of file test operators that can test various aspects of a file, the most basic being whether the file exists or not.

finger A program that provides information about users on an Internet host (possibly may include a user's personal information, such as project affiliation and schedule).

firewall A device placed on a network to prevent unauthorized traffic from entering the network.

flame Communicate in an abusive or absurd manner. Often occurs in newsgroup posts and e-mail messages.

flushing When data is output to a text file it is usually buffered to make processing more efficient, flushing forces any items in the buffer to be actually written to the file.

formats Perl allows the specification of formats to control the layout of text output.

forms Online data-entry sheets supported by some World Wide Web browsers.

frame relay A type of digital data communications protocol.

freeware Software that is made available by the author at no cost to anyone who wants it (although the author retains rights to the software).

FTP (File Transfer Protocol) An Internet communications protocol that allows you to transfer files between hosts on the Internet.

function A function is a set of commands that may be passed to some arguments and return a result.

gateway A device that interfaces two networks that use different protocols.

GID (**Group identifier**), a number representing the group that a process belongs to in the operating system.

gigabit Very high-speed (one billion bits per second) data communications.

gigabyte A unit of data storage approximately equal to one billion bytes of data.

global variables Variables that can be referred to anywhere within a package.

Gopher An application that allows you to access publicly available information on Internet hosts that provide Gopher service.

Gopherbook An application that uses an interface resembling a book to access Gopher servers.

grep A UNIX pattern matching utility.

GUI (Graphical User Interface) A computer interface based on graphical symbols rather than text. Windowing environments and Macintosh environments are GUIs.

gzip A file compression program originally designed to replace the UNIX compress utility.

hacking Originally referred to playing around with computer systems; now often used to indicate destructive computer activity.

hash lookup Find the value associated with a specified key in an associative array.

hash table A method used for implementing associative arrays, which allows the keys to be converted to numbers for internal storage purposes.

home page The document that your World Wide Web browser loads when it starts up. It should have links to other documents that you use frequently. Also, the main entry point to a site is sometimes called its home page (the default first page for that site).

hop-check A utility that allows you to find out how many routers are between your host and another Internet host. See also *traceroute*.

host address A unique number assigned to identify a host on the Internet (also called IP address or dot address). This address is usually represented as four numbers between 1 and 254 and separated by periods, for example, 192.58.107.230.

host name A unique name for a host that corresponds to the host address.

hosts Individual computers connected to the Internet; see also *nodes*.

hot list A list of your favorite World Wide Web sites that can be accessed quickly by your WWW browser.

HTML (Hypertext Markup Language) The formatting language that is used to create World Wide Web documents.

HTTP (Hypertext Transport Protocol) The communications protocol that allows WWW hypertext documents to be retrieved quickly.

hyperlinks See *links*.

hypertext An online document that has words or graphics containing links to other documents. Usually, selecting the link area on-screen (with a mouse or keyboard command) activates these links.

IEEE (Institute of Electrical and Electronics Engineers) The professional society for electrical and computer engineers.

IETF (Internet Engineering Task Force) A group of volunteers that helps develop Internet standards.

Internet The term used to describe all the worldwide interconnected TCP/IP networks.

Internet Explorer A Microsoft Windows 95 Web browser.

InterNIC The NSFNET manager sites on the Internet that provide information about the Internet.

IP (Internet Protocol) The communications protocol used by computers connected to the Internet.

IP address See *host address*.

IPC (**Inter-Process Communication**) Perl has a way to access the UNIX system for passing values between running processes.

ISO (International Standards Organization) An organization that sets worldwide standards in many different areas.

key In an associative array, a series of unique keys are associated with values.

LAN (Local Area Network) A network of computers that is limited to a (usually) small physical area, like a building.

leased line A dedicated phone line used for network communications.

library In Perl 4, the standard way to distribute code was in a library (accessed using the `require()` function); in Perl 5, modules are normally used, though libraries may still be used.

LIFO (**Last-In First-Out**) A queue where the last item placed in the queue is the first item processed when the queue is processed.

links The areas (words or graphics) in an HTML document that cause another document to be loaded when the user clicks them.

list A list is a series of values separated by commas; lists are often enclosed in parentheses to avoid ambiguity and these parentheses are often necessary.

list context This is the same as array context.

listproc Software that automates the management of electronic mailing lists. See also *LISTSERV*, *majordomo*, and *SmartList*.

LISTSERV Software that automates the management of electronic-mailing lists. See also *listproc*, *majordomo*, and *SmartList*.

local variables Local variables can only be accessed in the current block and in subroutines called from that block.

local host The computer you are currently using.

logical operators This term is used to mean Boolean operators, that is, those dealing with True/False values.

logon Provide a user ID and password to allow you to use the resources of a computer.

mailers Applications that let you read and send e-mail messages.

mailing list A service that forwards an e-mail message sent to it to everyone on a list, allowing a group of people to discuss a particular topic.

majordomo Software that automates the management of electronic mailing lists. See also *listproc*, *LISTSERV*, and *SmartList*.

man A UNIX command that provides information about the UNIX command entered in the parameter command. (The man command is short for manual entry.)

match A string that does fit a specified pattern.

metacharacters Characters that have a special meaning and so may need to be escaped to turn off that meaning.

MIME (Multi-Purpose Internet Mail Extensions) An extension to Internet mail that allows for the inclusion of non-textual data such as video and audio in e-mail.

modem An electronic device that allows digital computer data to be transmitted via analog phone lines.

moderator A person who examines all submissions to a newsgroup or mailing list and allows only those that meet certain criteria to be posted. Usually, the moderator makes sure that the topic is pertinent to the group and that the submissions aren't flames.

module The standard Perl 5 way to distribute libraries of functions.

Mosaic A graphical interface to the World Wide Web (WWW).

motd (**message of the day**) A message posted on some computer systems to let people know about problems or new developments.

my variables Perl 5 has a type of variable that is truly local to only the block in which it is declared, as distinct from local variables that can actually be accessed from subroutines called from the block.

namespace Variables names can have different scopes (such as global, local, and my) that determine which variable is being referred to at any point in a Perl program. The term namespace is used when describing how a variable name fits into this scheme (for example, a local variable in a subroutine is not in the package namespace).

netiquette Network etiquette conventions used in written communications, usually referring to UseNet newsgroup postings but also applicable to e-mail.

netnews A collective way of referring to the UseNet newsgroups.

Netscape A popular commercial World Wide Web browser.

network A number of computers physically connected to enable communication with one another.

newsgroups The electronic discussion groups of UseNet.

newsreaders Applications that let you read (and usually post) articles in UseNet newsgroups.

NFS (Network File System) A file system developed by Sun Microsystems that is now widely used on many different networks.

NIC (Network Interface Card) And add-on card to allow a machine to access a LAN (most commonly an ethernet card).

NIC (Network Information Center) A service that provides administrative information about a network.

NNTP (Network News Transport Protocol) The communications protocol that is used to send UseNet news on the Internet.

nodes Individual computers connected to a network; see also *hosts*.

NSFNET Network funded by the National Science Foundation, now the backbone of the Internet.

null character A character with the value 0.

null list An empty list represented as empty parentheses.

operand Argument to an operator (often an expression itself that must be evaluated first).

operator Usually a symbol that indicates that the relevant arguments (operands) are processed according to some rule and replaced with an appropriate result. Operators that are words are also allowed. This means that the distinction between a function and an operator is one based on the order of evaluation rather than a difference in what they do. In fact, in Perl 5, all functions can effectively be used as operators by omitting the parentheses.

package A unit of Perl code that determines the scope of the variables. Variables in a Perl program without any explicit package declaration are assumed to be in the package main.

packet The unit of data transmission on the Internet. A packet consists of the data being transferred with additional overhead information, such as the transmitting and receiving addresses.

packet switching The communications technology that the Internet is based on, where data being sent between computers is transmitted in packets.

parallel Means of communication in which digital data is sent multiple bits at a time, with each simultaneous bit being sent over a separate line.

parameter Means the same as argument.

pattern An expression defining a set of strings that match the pattern and a set that do not.

PDIAL A list of mailing lists maintained by Stephanie da Silva (**arielle@taronga.com**), periodically posted to the **news.answers**, **news.announce.newusers**, and **news.lists** UseNet newsgroups.

peer-to-peer Internet services that can be offered and accessed by anyone, without requiring a special server.

Perl (**Practical Extraction and Report Language**) a language well suited to text file processing as well as other tasks.

PGP (Pretty Good Privacy) An application that allows you to send and receive encrypted e-mail.

PID Process identifier, a number indicating the number assigned by the operating system to that process.

ping A utility that sends out a packet to an Internet host and waits for a response (used to check if a host is up).

pipe The concept in an operating system where the output of one program is fed into the input of another.

Pipeline A complete Internet service package.

POP (Point of Presence) Indicates availability of a local access number to a public data network.

port (hardware) A physical channel on a computer that allows you to communicate with other devices (printers, modems, disk drives, and so on).

port (network) An address to which incoming data packets are sent. Special ports can be assigned to send the data directly to a server (FTP, Gopher, WWW, telnet, or e-mail) or other specific program.

post To send a message to a UseNet newsgroup.

postmaster An address to which you can send questions about a site (asking if a user has an account there or if they sell a particular product, for example).

PPP (Point-To-Point Protocol) A driver that allows you to use a network communications protocol over a phone line, used with TCP/IP to allow you to have a dial-in Internet host.

pragma A Perl 5 module whose real purpose is to act as a compile time directive rather than supply any functions (for example, the integer module that switches to integer arithmetic).

precedence The order in which operators are evaluated is based on their precedence.

procedure In some languages a distinction is made between subroutines that do not return a value (procedures) and those that do (functions). Perl itself does not make such distinctions, though the term may be used.

process In multitasking operating systems such as UNIX, many programs may be run at once and each one as it is running is called a process.

protocol The standard that defines how computers on a network communicate with one another.

public domain software Software that is made available by the author to anyone who wants it. (In this case, the author gives up all rights to the software.)

recursion When a subroutine makes a call to itself.

regular expressions A way of specifying a pattern so that some strings match the pattern and some strings do not. Parts of the matching pattern can be marked for use in operations such as substitution.

repeater Device that allows you to extend the length of your network by amplifying and repeating the information it receives.

remote Pertaining to a host on the network other than the computer you now are using.

remote host A host on the network other than the computer you currently are using.

rlogin A UNIX command that allows you to log on to a remote computer.

RFC (Request for Comments) A document submitted to the Internet governing board to propose Internet standards or to document information about the Internet.

router Equipment that receives an Internet packet and sends it to the next machine in the destination path.

scalar A type of Perl variable that is not an array, this includes all integer, floating-point, and string variables in Perl; scalar variable names begin with the $ sign.

scalar context A scalar value is required.

script A Perl program is often called script as it is an interpreted set of instructions in a text file (line a UNIX shell script).

scope The scope of a variable determines whether the variable name can be seen from various parts of a Perl program (see *global*, *local*, and *my*).

sed A UNIX editing utility.

serial Means of communication in which digital data is sent one bit at a time over a single physical line.

server Provider of a service. Also often refers to a piece of hardware or software that provides access to information requested from it. See also *client*.

server-side include (SSI) A command that directs the server to run a program, usually in the Perl programming language. SSIs are server-specific.

shareware Software that is made available by the author to anyone who wants it, with a request to send the author a nominal fee if the software is used on a regular basis.

shell The UNIX command interpreter (you often have a choice from a number of different shells).

signal A means of passing information between the operating system and a running process, the process can trap the signal and respond accordingly.

signature A personal sign-off used in e-mail and newsgroup posts, often contained in a file and automatically appended to the mail or post. Often contains organization affiliation and pertinent personal information.

site A group of computers under a single administrative control.

SLIP (Serial Line Internet Protocol) A way of running TCP/IP via the phone lines to allow you to have a dialup Internet host.

SmartList Software that automates the management of electronic-mailing lists. See also *listproc*, *LISTSERV*, and *majordomo*.

smiley face An ASCII drawing such as :-) (look at it sideways) used to help indicate an emotion in a message. Also called emoticon.

SMTP (Simple Mail Transport Protocol) The accepted communications protocol standard for exchange of e-mail between Internet hosts.

SNMP (Simple Network Management Protocol) A communications protocol used to control and monitor devices on a network.

socket A means of network communications via special entities; Perl allows direct access to the UNIX C socket mechanism.

string A sequence of characters.

subscribe Become a member of a mailing list or newsgroup; also refers to obtaining Internet provider services.

subscript The index number used to specify an element in an array.

substring A contiguous part of a string, starting at a certain character and continuing for a certain length.

surfing Jumping from host to host on the Internet to get an idea of what can be found. Also used to refer to briefly examining a number of different UseNet newsgroups.

syntax A statement that contains programming code.

T1 Communications lines operating at 1.544M/sec.

T3 Communications lines operating at 45M/sec.

tag A slang reference for commands that are part of HTML. See also *HTML*.

tainted A means in Perl of flagging variables as untrustworthy because the value has been input by a non-trusted source (this allows the development of secure programs for applications such as Web server programs reading user input).

tar (tape archive program) A UNIX-based program that creates packages of directory structures.

TCP (Transmission Control Protocol) The network protocol used by hosts on the Internet.

telnet A program that allows remote logon to another computer.

terminal emulation Running an application that lets you use your computer to interface with a command-line account on a remote computer, as if you were connected to the computer with a terminal.

thread All messages in a newsgroup or mailing list pertaining to a particular topic.

toggle Alternate between two possible values.

token ring A network protocol for LAN.

traceroute A utility that allows you to find out how many routers are between your host and another Internet host. See also *hop-check*.

traffic The information flowing through a network.

UID User identifier, a number representing a user account (all files and processes in UNIX are associated with the owner's UID).

unary operator An operator with one operand.

UNIX An operating system used on many Internet hosts.

upload Move a file from your local computer to a remote computer.

URL (Universal Resource Locator) Used to specify the location and name of a World Wide Web document. You can also specify other Internet services available from WWW browsers, for example, **http://www.nsf.gov** or **gopher://gopher2.tc.umn.edu**, or **ftp://ftp.funet.fi/pub/languages/perl/CPAN/**.

UseNet A collection of computer discussion groups that are read all over the world.

user name The ID used to log on to a computer.

UUCP (UNIX to UNIX Copy Protocol) An early transfer protocol for UNIX machines that required having one machine call the other one on the phone.

UUDecode A program that lets you construct binary data that was UUEncoded.

UUEncode A program that lets you send binary data through e-mail.

variable A storage place in memory used in a program while it is running to store values that may be altered by the program.

viewers Applications that are used to display non-text files, such as graphics, sound, and animation.

virus A computer program that covertly enters a system by means of a legitimate program, usually doing damage to the system; compare to *worm*.

VMS (Virtual Memory System) An operating system used on hosts made by Digital Equipment Corporation.

VRML (Virtual Reality Modeling Language) An experimental language that lets you display 3D objects in Web documents.

WAIS (Wide Area Information Servers) A system for searching and retrieving documents from participating sites.

WAN (Wide Area Network) A network of computers that are geographically dispersed.

Web Chat An application that allows you to carry on live conversations over the World Wide Web.

Web Crawler A Web search tool.

WHOIS A service that lets you look up information about Internet hosts and users.

World Wide Web (WWW or Web) A hypertext-based system that allows browsing of available Internet resources.

worm A computer program that invades other computers over a network, usually non-destructively; compare to *virus*.

X-modem A communication protocol that lets you transfer files over a serial line. See also *Y-modem* and *Z-modem*.

yacc A UNIX utility program for generating compilers based on a grammar (Yet Another Compiler Compiler).

Y-modem A communication protocol that lets you transfer files over a serial line. See also *X-modem* and *Z-modem*.

Z-modem A communication protocol that lets you transfer files over a serial line. See also *X-modem* and *Y-modem*.

ZIP Probably the singular most popular file compression and archive program for PCs.

INDEX

Symbols

A

B

C

D

G

H

M

N

O

P

Q

R

S

W

X-Y-Z

```
While (<FH>) {     # read 1 line at
                     a time
  $line = $_    }

$line =~ /__/   Compare pattern
```